Quietly, HE Speaks

By: Carla J. Akin

Copyright © 2006 by Carla J. Akin

Quietly, HE Speaks
by Carla J. Akin

Printed in the United States of America
This book is printed on acid-free paper.

ISBN 1-59781-880-1

All rights reserved solely by the author. This book is a work of non-fiction. Unless otherwise noted, the author and the publisher make no explicit guarantees as to the accuracy of the information contained in this book and in some cases; names of people and places have been altered to protect their privacy. No part of this book may be reproduced, stored in a retrieval system, or transmitted by any means without the written permission of the author. The views expressed in this book are not necessarily those of the publisher.

Unless otherwise indicated, Bible quotations are taken from the International Version of the Bible. Copyright © 2005 by Zondervan Publishers, The Bible Gateway and King James Version, Nelson Publishers.

www.xulonpress.com

June 17, 2010

Jimmy,

May God Bless You and it is so great knowing you.

Love
Carla Akin

Table of Contents

Dedication vii
Foreword ix
Prologue xi
Acknowledgment xv

Chapter One—His Character 19

Chapter Two—Radical Thinking 49

Chapter Three—His Message 75

Chapter Four—A Call for Holy Living 101

Chapter Five—His Warnings 121

Chapter Six—The Heavenly City 151

Epilogue 167

Final Words for Thought 173

Dedication

This book is dedicated to all whose walk is with the Lord, as an encouragement to them! This book is lovingly dedicated to my family and friends. One day we will sit around the Throne of GOD and be together forever! I am awaiting the Marriage Supper of the Lamb!

My heartfelt dedication to Mary Lou Stanford. Thank You for believing in me and reading through the many revisions of this book and seeing it through to its completion. Lu Lu, you are my forever friend and business partner for life! I love you!

Special thanks to my dear friend, Carolyn (Ida) Millar for reading the prophesies in this book and inspiring me with her poem, which I have included in the Foreword. I am blessed to have Carolyn in my life!

To all my Readers, may you find the heartbeat of GOD in these pages and dedicate your life to living for the one who is worth living for, Jesus Christ!

Lastly, to Jessica Nicole, my precious, loving daughter! Your spirit of sweetness is a fragrant aroma in our home and I love you more than you will ever know! I thank GOD each day for the precious gift of YOU! Your artwork is stunning and the inspiration for the cover of this book will be enjoyed by many. You have only just begun!!

Foreword

My friend, Carla J. Akin inspired me with the prophesies written in this book. I wrote this poem about what I felt, and received from reading what she has received from the Lord. This poem is my gift to HIM.

> The Prophet Had Written Them With Hand
> His word's jumped out at me.
> The prophet had written them with hand.
> I saw the cross – rugged and old.
> I saw stripes upon His back.
> The stripes were red and waiving -
> Like the stripes upon the flag;
>
> Save a soul. Remove a stripe.
> Oh, yes, I've saved souls.
>
> But of late -
> until now,
> I've had no reason,
> no care.
>
> If only I could remove some more of His pain.
>
> Please, I pray this very day.
> Help me heal His pain.
>
> Believe in HIM, I pray!
>
> Ida Millar
> © 11/23/05

Prologue

*Q*uietly, HE speaks. Do you hear His voice?
I hope you will discover that this book touches your heart, as these messages have touched mine and made such an incredible difference in my walk with GOD. HE quietly speaks to me and I offer His messages to a hurting world, to inspire you to find hope in the midst of all your tomorrows!

The messages below, like all the messages included in this book, are addressed to me, as "My beloved." Read them with an open heart, as if He is speaking to you. He loves you so very much!

Please know that GOD is always with us, and He is only a knock away from the door of your heart!

June 30, 2005
5:45 a.m.

My beloved,

Keep seeking me in the early hours, though your physical body is sleepy and not alert, your spirit is receptive to hear my words and you do well to listen for my voice. I know it would be easier for you to ignore my gentle voice and to continue to sleep, yet your heart yearns for the deeper things of me. You are a truth seeker and you long to know me intimately.

It is as Pastor said, very few seek me, but only the chosen; they attend church. Many do not even open up their Bibles and read my WORD. They know not me, only an idea of me.

I have so much to give and share with my children, if only they took the time to draw near to me.

I am in control of all things and yet I can be persuaded, just as an earthly Father can be persuaded by his own children; however, I cannot go against what is in my written Word.

I am not an unreasonable GOD; I see the pressures of life are everywhere. People are breaking from the daily demands on them.

This should not be; they can give their burdens to me. I will give them my peace. It takes trust and obedience, mixed with wisdom to have a close walk with me. This is an ongoing process and does not happen overnight.

Just as you carefully cultivate your earthly friendships, the same is true for our relationship. I am not so different from mankind; you are created in my image.

I will show you many more mysteries of me in time. For now, walk in obedience to me and keep seeking me.

Shalom, my precious daughter.

As you just read, He longs to speak to those who will listen to Him! GOD loves to fellowship with His people, who are called by His name.

Did you know that you are called by Him?

Do you realize how much He loves You?

He is the voice over many waters. His is the voice speaking to You throughout all of nature. Do you feel nudges in your spirit about "right" and "wrong"?

He is the life giver, the one who can meet all our needs! He holds the world in His mighty hands; He holds all our tomorrows and so much more!

He exists and He is waiting for You to draw near to Him.

He created the Heavens and the earth, the day and the night, the planets, the stars, the trees, and the animals. In doing so, He put everything under man's dominion. On the sixth day of creation,

He created mankind in His own image, and on the seventh day He rested from all His work.

Everything He created is for our good pleasure and He has a perfect plan for us!

Are you hungry to discover there is a GOD and that He is near to You?

He has a perfect plan and He is waiting for You to come to Him. GOD is patient, and He wants to fellowship with all humanity, not just a select group of people. Do you want to discover the plan He has for your life?

He wants you to hear His voice and to trust Him to give you the love and acceptance that perhaps you haven't found in the world.

He is that gap, that person who will accept you, just as you are! GOD will meet you right where you are at. If you don't believe in GOD at this point on your journey of life, open your heart. He asks that you have an open mind and let Him guide you into all truth.

I cry out to GOD and He hears my prayers. I love the Lord and I pray that you will also love Him, with your whole heart and soul.

Quietly, HE speaks to mankind, and He will speak to you too! Are you listening for His voice?

GOD wants to talk to You!

Let's take this spiritual journey together and discover the voice of GOD.

Acknowledgment

*T*here is only one whom I can possibly acknowledge for this book, which is my Lord and Savior, Jesus Christ. He is the one who saved me and changed me in ways that I could not ever dream of.

March 6, 2005
4:50 a.m.

Lord Jesus,

In the silent stillness I hear your voice as one crying out in the night. I know that I sit in your presence, the calmness and peace is overwhelming. While the world sleeps in sweet slumber, you gently whisper the secret things to me. I am your servant, my life revolves around you and there are not false idols in which I seek an audience.

Jesus, you are all that I live for, in your presence there is fullness of joy and to live and serve you is beyond measure of anything I could compare it to. Our relationship is special.

People think it strange when I tell of our early morning encounters, they do not understand. Many want the same, but they are not willing to pay the price.

Are you willing to pay the price?

JESUS will love you more deeply and more real than any human ever could. It is beyond our human capabilities to love like Jesus loves, unless we are born of Him and have dedicated our heart and souls to Him. Only then, can we attempt to love each other like Jesus loves us.

For all the ways that Jesus has loved me, I thank Him and I give Him all the Glory and Honor forever!

I thank Him for healing my body many times!

I thank Him for the many miracles in my life and I thank Him for my children. I thank Him for dying on a brutal cross to give me the precious gift of an eternal life with Him in Heaven.

I can never repay Him for the love He has so graciously bestowed on me.

Jesus Christ, "Yeshua" is my all-in-all, and I pray by the end of this book, you too will love Him most deeply. My heart is full to overflowing.

[105] Your word is a lamp to my feet and a light for my path.
Psalm 119:105 NIV

Thank You Jesus Christ for everything!

Chapter One

His Character

¹ I love the LORD, for He heard my voice; He heard my cry for mercy.
² Because He turned His ear to me, I will call on Him as long as I live.
³ The cords of death entangled me, the anguish of the grave came upon me; I was overcome by trouble and sorrow.
⁴ Then I called on the name of the LORD "O LORD, save me!"
⁵ The LORD is gracious and righteous; our GOD is full of compassion.
⁶ The LORD protects the simple hearted; when I was in great need, He saved me.
⁷ Be at rest once more, O my soul, for the LORD has been good to you.
⁸ For you, O LORD, have delivered my soul from death, my eyes from tears, and my feet from stumbling;
⁹ That I may walk before the LORD in the land of the living.
¹⁰ I believed; therefore I said, "I am greatly afflicted."
¹¹ And in my dismay I said, "All men are liars."
¹² How can I repay the LORD for all His goodness to me?
¹³ I will lift up the cup of salvation and call on the name of the LORD.
¹⁴ I will fulfill my vows to the LORD in the presence of all His people.
¹⁵ Precious in the sight of the LORD is the death of His Saints.

¹⁶ O LORD, truly I am your servant; I am your servant, the son of your maidservant; you have freed me from my chains.
¹⁷ I will sacrifice a thank offering to you and call on the name of the LORD.
¹⁸ I will fulfill my vows to the LORD in the presence of all His people;
¹⁹ In the courts of the house of the LORD, in your midst, O Jerusalem. Praise the LORD.

Psalm 116 NIV

As beautiful as these words have been for centuries, they are sweetness to my ears as I feel the love from King David, the writer of this Psalm. It is amazing how something written so long ago can still be felt in the hearts of many in today's world.

I have discovered the goodness of GOD and I as I share Him with you, I pray you will too!

So, let's discover GOD in the following pages and what He desires you to learn of Him.

Most of us have heard the story of the sacrifice of Jesus' death on the cross. It has been written in our history books for centuries and etched on the face of America.

Jesus was born of a virgin mother, Mary, and was raised as a Carpenter. He learned the trade from His earthly father, Joseph. Scholars tell us that although Jesus lived on earth for 33 years, His ministry was a very short three years.

What an impact one man made on a society that has been changed forever, since He left Heaven and came to dwell among men and women.

Talk about real character! Jesus gave up His throne in Heaven, and was willing to be created as a man and be born as a baby, trusting a 14 year-old girl to raise Him as Her son. Jesus demonstrated the purest of love and total trust in mankind.

Not only that, but He was willing to suffer so much, living as a man, but being GOD in power and might. One can probably never understand this completely and I trust that while we are here on earth, it is not meant for us to comprehend, only believe!

I often wonder if GOD ever regretted creating us.

Jesus, in the Hebrew language is "Yeshua" and in the messages that GOD speaks to me, He often refers to His Son's name as such.

¹² For the word of GOD is living and active. Sharper than any double-edged sword, it penetrates even to dividing soul and spirit, joints and marrow; it judges the thoughts and attitudes of the heart.
¹³ Nothing in all creation is hidden from GOD's sight. Everything is uncovered and laid bare before the eyes of Him to whom we must give account.

Hebrews 4:12-13 NIV

We can encounter GOD and hear His voice, if we repent of our sins and accept Jesus into our heart.

Just as the above Scripture reassures us, He is always watching over us! He is interceding for us and we are in His sight and nothing is hidden from Him.

So, do you want to hear from GOD?

Then you must get still and silent before Him. It is not some mystical mystery, but rather a simple process, one of a surrendered heart, pure towards GOD.

It is a sweet sound in my mind and I live to dwell in His presence.

I find it much easier if all distractions are eliminated in my secret place, so for my time of fellowship, I even turn off my praise and worship music while we are fellowshipping together.

Singing praises to GOD with praise and worship music is necessary to bring about the LORD's presence. GOD promises His children that He delights in the praises of His people.

If you are searching for the truth on your walk of life, you have found a place to stop and meditate on the truth of GOD's Word included in this book and in the Bible.

It is the normal in our world today to get so busy with our lives, which are filled with many activities and distractions, and not reflect on GOD and His peace that He longs to share with us.

We each have to make a conscious choice or decision to calendar time in each day to listen to GOD. I must admit, this is a struggle for me, and perhaps the reason He wakes me up from my sleep in the early morning hours. I fall asleep talking to GOD, but I am always in sweet anticipation of His hour when He wakes me up.

I am most thankful and humbled He even bothers with me!

In this time of awakening, I feel a gentle nudge and then I hear those same sweet words, "My beloved" and I know it is time to grab my pen and paper. Sometimes, He is speaking so quickly I have to scribble to the point of my hand cramping up, but the gentleman that He is, He stops and pauses until I catch up. I am learning to write faster and faster!

He keeps me just awake enough to pencil the words, and then He quickly puts me back to sleep, just as gently and sweetly as when He woke me up.

Once the morning arrives, I am filled with sweet anticipation to read the message He gave me through the night. I am always filled with awe that I don't fully remember the message from the night before; however, I am sure He plans it this way to keep my opinions out, so I hear only what He wants said.

GOD does not need my "two cents," just my obedience and my surrendered body to be used for His Will.

Recently, GOD told me, *"if it's not 100% obedience, it is not obedience."* Wow, so pure and simple and yet many of us neglect this simple truth.

Please be encouraged, GOD does whisper His heart to those who love Him. He speaks to the silent, stillness in your soul and He is waiting for you!

If you have never encountered the voice of GOD, please understand that HE is no respecter of persons and He will speak to you, just repent and seek Him!

As we read below, GOD warns us of the trials we will go through in this life. The good news, He will also equip us for this walk and be with us on our journey.

September 20, 2005
3:50 a.m.

My beloved,

Many are the plans I have set before you!

You are on the narrow road, but be careful and use wisdom so you do not move over onto the wide road. This walk I command of my Saints is not an easy one and it is filled with trials and temptations. I will equip my people so they will not perish in the Lake of Fire, but they will heed the calling on their lives.

Many are slumbering and not giving me the time I require of them to fulfill the calling on their lives.

The time is short and I've sent my prophets out into the world to give my wake-up calls.

Many do not heed the messengers I send forth. It will be to their demise. They eat, drink and party as though they are of the world. My people need to rise up at this last hour and preach the gospel of my Son, Jesus. He sacrificed so much for them and they live as if He has made no difference.

You cannot do any of this in your own talents and gifts! To save the lost you must carry my anointing, which comes with a price. If you want to serve me well and do my will, you must lay down your life, your plans and take up my plans for your life, otherwise, I have no use for you.

I will no longer entertain your plans; the time is too short to play Church with me.

If you are lukewarm, I will spit you out of my mouth.

I am a living GOD with everlasting love and kindness, but if you saw people in a burning building, wouldn't you rush in to save them? It is the same with people following their wicked ways and they don't recognize they are in a spiritual burning building. They will perish in the Lake of Fire if someone doesn't take my gospel to them. They do not understand the condition they are in and it takes my servants to tell them of the Savior.

Be strong and of good courage my children, I am always with you! Open your mouths and I will fill it with words from the Holy

Spirit. He is being poured out over the world to equip the Saints in this last hour.

Gird up your loins and be about your Father's business, it has a Kingly reward in Heaven with much beauty no eyes have ever seen. The peace you will dwell in will be like nothing you've ever known. I will wipe away all your tears and you will discover that every trial you endured was not even worthy to be counted when you see my plan come to fruition in your life.

I don't want my children to be filled with grief when they realize the hour they live and they did not serve me whole heartily, that is why I am sending my messengers into the world now for you to heed my words.

I have no desire to harm anyone, but when given a free will, many will make the wrong choice. They cannot understand my love for them unless they accept Jesus into their hearts. He will then deposit a right spirit in them and a measure of faith so they can feel and receive my love for them.

I so long to bless my children, if only they would let go of what they possess and their precious agenda's and let me give them a better way.

People need to rid themselves of false idols in their lives. It will consume much energy to worry about their possessions, which can be gone in an instant. Store up treasures in Heaven, where the thieves cannot reach it and where you will be greatly rewarded.

Do not lean on your own understandings, but in all your ways acknowledge me and I will direct your paths and show you my great reward for you, my faithful servants.

No small or larger act of giving do I not see. I see everything and all that you do is not hidden from my sight. I see your hearts, your thoughts and your motives. Nothing in all creation is hidden from me.

Continue seeking me while I may be found. As the battle intensifies in the heavenly realms, the storms will become greater and more intense.

Shalom, my beloved.
It is as a mirror.

February 23, 2005
3:24 a.m.

Be strong, keep the obedience, do not slack back, now is the time of battle in the heavenly places!

I need my Saints to pray, it is for their good that my Angels do battle over them. Do they not see the sacrifices my Angels serve daily to protect them? If it were not for these faithful ones, many would have already perished.

My Angels stand ready to fight, they are not to be worshipped, but I am to be worshipped. The Angels are my soldiers, they obey me. Man goes his own way, he does not obey, why do I still contend with him?

I want to fellowship, yet they do not listen for my voice. My heart is heavy; I have so much love to give if only they would listen.

They only listen in trouble, the earth is heavy burdened, its storms are the beginning my beloved, watch as my wrath continues.

Shalom.

The preceding message shows us that GOD is overseeing our lives and He protects us. It also shows us that He is Sovereign and He gives us a warning of the earth's burdens and what will come upon the earth in the future.

In the following message He again reinforces the warning that many need to follow Him and that He is a rewarder of those who seek Him, as I have chosen to do. I have dedicated myself to Him and He has answered my prayers of having a heart for winning the souls of the lost. This is one such message of encouragement to me, and I hope it is of encouragement to you as well.

March 11, 2005

My beloved,

I am well pleased with you. You search for the deeper things of my Kingdom. You warn the people, you have obeyed my commands. I will equip you to complete the book. I am well pleased, my words will not return void. You do well to use my words to warn the people. They will know and recognize it as such.

Your reward will be great. The crown I will place on you will be for your good pleasure. Your tears, your hurt, I placed some of my heart in you tonight, you are changed. I am trusting you with my thoughts and my people. You are beginning to carry some of my burdens. Now you see the pain, now you understand the sacrifice, my people are perishing! It is good that you are pressing in; the time is at hand.

You are growing fast; I will continue to mold you. You are learning Satan's devices, I see you breaking the fiery darts off of you. You are doing what I have been teaching you. I am pouring out My Spirit in you. You will carry the power you desire. You will heal the people; you will cast out demons in my name. You will be of great use to me. I love you, my beloved. I see how tired you are. I will give you rest and comfort you. Sleep my beloved.

Shalom, my precious one.

The message below reveals GOD's heart and His sorrow over the people He created. His character is one of integrity and He keeps giving us second and third chances to seek Him. GOD is so interested in your very life, that as you read below, you will see He promises me of a wonderful future, if I will seek Him first and do His work, and He will bless me for it. It is good to know that none of this work is in vain.

April 4, 2005
1:30 a.m.

My beloved,

Worship me and continue to seek me! You do well to encourage others to sit and listen for me. Not all will hear my voice; they are an obstinate people filled with pride. Do not be deceived by them, they are wolves in sheep's clothing; you do good to stay your distance. Do not throw your pearls to pigs.

I have heard the cries of your prayers and I will not forsake you. You have been obedient to me and I will give you the desires of your heart. All will be accomplished in my time.

Rest in me, for now you are my beloved bride and I love you with a consuming fire; I am not ready to give you to the anointed one. Your time will come and you will be one, yet while it is still called today, rejoice and seek me in all your ways. I will prosper you, I will lead you. Follow me my child and I will exalt you to a high level and I know you wrestle with your own unworthiness.

Why do you think it impossible to have the home you truly desire? I have placed those desires into your heart and it gives me great joy to lift you up and place you in a castle where others will know and marvel at my hand upon you.

Do not settle for less than I am willing to give you.

I do all these things for your good pleasure.

The harvest is ready, my children are perishing, I have looked throughout the earth for obedient children, and they are so few! You have been chosen; I see your heart and know you love me. You have done well and I will greatly reward you. Many cannot understand, they see not your heart, only your mistakes. Do not worry, they persecuted my Son and spit and mocked Him, they never value those I place to save them.

How foolish are the people of the world. I grow weary with their disobedience. Multitudes want the blessings, but they didn't want my Son. Few think about how He suffered for them.

Carla, you heed the voice of my Holy Spirit and you understand the deeper things of me. Many think you are a fool, relax and understand that is how it should be. To the ones that are lost and seeking, they will recognize you are mine. Do not be discouraged when you hear not my voice, I am always with you my child and often I use the silence to grow and stretch you. Each trial of pain and loneliness makes you stronger. The enemy cannot have you, though he is increasingly trying.

You are my beloved, in whom I am well pleased. Continue in me and I will give you the desires of your heart.

Shalom, my beloved.

May 1, 2005

My beloved,

Many things the wicked does not understand about me. I am the Alpha and Omega, the beginning and the end. I do not change like the shifting winds, my Word stands alone.

I rise up and lift those up whom I choose, and I spit out of my mouth those whom I choose.

It is not to them that I need to explain myself; they are wicked and full of lies to mislead my holy ones. I will have the last word! You will see the mighty acts that I will bring to pass in your life and in Jessica's life.

You are mine; you do not hear from the evil one, you are in obedience to me.

Rejoice and worship me, I love to see your adoration and devotion to me. You know my heart, keep preaching the word, it will not return void; you will minister to the multitudes.

Many are coming into the Kingdom through you. You will be rewarded greatly, my beloved.

I know this walk has not been easy. I know many think you are a fool. Remember they are dogs at the foot of your table; do not be concerned, the foolish and wicked will never understand, they know not my ways.

Just as my Servant Job was rewarded 100 fold, you and Jessica also will be.

You will have the desires of your heart because you will give me all the glory and I will return it back to you. I will not take the anointed one away from you, even though you meant your heart's cry. It was enough for me to know you were willing to give him up for me.

The anointed one needs you! You are my chosen for him, so together you can accomplish the great and mighty things I have laid before you during the harvest of souls which are laid before you.

I love you my child. Rest in me, I give you Glory and Honor. Shalom, now and forever.

I will be with you in the storm that is soon to come. I will be with you always.

Again, as we have just read, GOD is Sovereign and He will bring about judgment in His timing.

Although He judges us, He keeps encouraging us to seek Him and by His words He shows His love for us. He cares about even the smallest detail of our lives, just as He continues to encourage me about my life.

May 26, 2005
4:30 a.m.

My beloved,

You do well to wait upon me and I will show you great and mighty things. I will open doors for you so you can tell of my love and faithfulness to you, one of my former lost sheep.

Rest where you are and be blessed. I will promote and move you in my time; for the present stay where I have placed you.

Remember that all things work together for good to those who love the LORD. I will cause even your enemies to rise up and bless you.

You do well to hang onto your faith and the joy I've placed inside you is a mighty weapon to use against the enemy of your soul. Although he keeps trying to get you to stop worshipping me, his attempts continue to fail. Stay strong and stay the course.

Walk each day towards me and I will continue to guide you.

Stay where I have placed you, do not move, you are there to be a light and the devil wants to isolate you. Keep testing the spirits and the voices you hear. Test every thought and take it captive to the Word of GOD.

Satan wants to destroy you, but my hand is upon your life and I will protect you from his schemes.

The time is close at hand for your deliverance. Stay strong and see what great things I will do for my daughters.

You and Jessica are so precious to me and I long to be your Father to you both.

Sleep well, my precious child.

Shalom.

Stay where I place you refers to the timing of a move I was contemplating. I was unsure and this was His answer to my prayer to Him for guidance. I try to always consult with GOD on every aspect of my life, especially something as important as where to live.

June 1, 2005
4:30 a.m.

My beloved,

You are seeing Satan beef up his attempts to discourage you. You do well to keep your peace through the storm. My hand is upon you and Jessica will be protected from the schemes of the devil.

I will handle all things, just take your hands off and surrender to me so I can do battle for you. Stop carrying the burdens; give them to me! Praise me with your whole heart. Focus on me and do not look at the natural. You are my child and I have much to teach you.

You must unload the burdens and praise me!

Your body is subject to illness because of the heavy load, this should not be so. I have made all provisions for you to enjoy a healthy and long life, yet you suffer because you are not surrendering your burdens to me. Surrender Carla; tell me of your thoughts and worries. Let go of the bitterness you feel in your heart.

I do not change like the shifting shadows. I am the same yesterday, today and tomorrow!

Time cannot contain me, I dwell in everlasting light unapproachable by man in their earthly tents.

Only the heavenly bodies can dwell in my sight. My power is too strong for your earthen clay vessels to withstand my glory.

I long to give you my love; that is why I've sent my Holy Spirit to comfort and love, there is less power and your earthly body can house Him. He speaks to you only what I tell Him, to comfort or correct you. Do not grieve my Holy Spirit with grief, sorrow and disbelief.

Remember to hold onto your joy and praise me. It pleases the Holy Spirit and is a sweet aroma to me.

I enjoy the sacrifice of praise when my people are in the midst of the storm.

I will show you more mysteries, for now rest my child. Remember to obey me and cast your burdens on me.

Shalom, my precious one.

Sometimes I have to be almost "hit over the head" to get it. Although I know that GOD promises to carry our burdens, I am often guilty of trying to figure out my life without bothering the LORD.

The LORD GOD does not want us living independently of Him. He wants us to rely and consult Him, just as we want to be consulted and involved in our own children's life. This message was a strong reminder to me of this fact and I hope it speaks to your heart if you also wrestle with this.

Each time I encounter GOD, I come away changed and I am in awe that He cares for any of us, so much so that He gave His only begotten Son, Jesus to live and dwell with mankind for a short 33 years on earth.

As you have just read in the previous messages, it is a testimony of GOD's character, His everlasting love and devotion to the people He created.

These messages are for you, as an encouragement to know that GOD sees all things!

He sees your heart's desires and your longing. He will meet you where you are at and these messages are a testimony to the depth of His love for us. Although He dwells in Heaven and earth is His footstool, we are His, and GOD loves each one of us the same! He is no respecter of persons.

We are never too far from GOD's grace and His abundant love. He searches the hearts and minds of all His creation and He is searching for YOU.

June 16, 2005
2:45 a.m.

My beloved,

The praises of my people pleased me tonight, to see so many with their surrendered hearts. I can move and mold a surrendered vessel. I long to tell them the mysteries of the heart; once they draw near to me.

Many are the devices of Satan to cause distractions among my people. Quarrels, financial bondage and the like keep my body in turmoil and looking at their trials, all the while, one by one, the people are dying without Jesus as their Savior.

My workers are like the ostrich, keeping their head in the sand and worrying about their own problems, while the people around them are perishing. The fight is real; Satan has blinded so many, even those who call themselves a member of my body.

Keep writing. I want a book that speaks to the people from my heart. A newer version of the one you read earlier. I will equip you. You have proven your obedience to me.

I will meet with you and give you the words. Write my words to the people.

Shalom, my beloved one.

GOD wants all of us to know how much He loves us and to watch for the devices of our enemy, Satan. With knowledge can we be equipped to look out for the traps of the devil and they are everywhere! That is why Jesus came to the earth, to destroy the devil and his demons and to set us free from the curse of death and Hades.

I encourage you to seek and wait upon Him so you can experience His sweet voice. Please remember as I've told you above, that although these writings were written to me, they are for everyone!

Once you begin this journey, in the first few days or weeks, you may not hear anything. But, don't give up, keep pressing into His heart and keep talking to Him. I know He is listening to you!

Sometimes He will test us to see how much time we will sacrifice before Him, before He will open up the dialogue He has been waiting to pour into your spirit.

He is always worth the wait!

It may seem very awkward in the beginning to feel like you are talking to the air, but remember, GOD is everywhere and He is listening! Since GOD created all things of nature, just as He created everyone, including You, He knows your heartbeat and He longs to tell you of His love for You.

No one understands you more than GOD, nor does anyone love you more than Him!

> [11] "For I know the plans I have for you," declares the LORD, "plans to prosper you and not to harm you, plans to give you hope and a future."
> [12] Then you will call upon me and come and pray to me, and I will listen to you.
> [13] You will seek me and find me when you seek me with all your heart.
>
> Jeremiah 29:11-13 NIV

I sought out the LORD for years before I was really cognizant of His presence. I would often go out into nature, especially around lakes or mountains and I would feel closeness. It was not readily apparent to me in the beginning that this closeness was GOD. I was not sensitive to His voice, but I wanted desperately for Him to hear the cries of my heart, and now I realize He did. You will see that as you read the following message.

June 5, 2005
4:30 a.m.

My beloved,

Continue in me and keep seeking me and praising me! Isaiah 55 speaks to you; continue to study these WORDS that I have brought to you.

All things were created by me for my good pleasure; it is wonderful to see you enjoying the works of my hands. The trees praise me, just as you do.

I am well pleased that you sought the presence of me in nature, it is where I can speak to your spirit in a different way and I can come close to brush against you. The wind is like my breath breathing on you and it is refreshing to your spirit and soul.

Keep connecting to me and teach Jessica, although she has great revelation of me, it is good to teach her the elementary teachings so in the hardships of her adult life, she will remember.

Keep encouraging each other and do not quarrel. I did not create you to argue with each other. You are my children, be good to each other. Jessica has a sweet spirit, she is dealing with many things, help her to learn respect, but do not break her spirit.

Divine appointments will continue to come your way. You are blessed and I will continue to bless you. Your heart pleases me and your willingness to obey is good. I can trust you with more of me as you continue to prove to me you will heed my words and not look to the left or the right.

Stay the course and walk according to my leading. Few walk in this obedience and are led by me. You will receive great rewards for your obedience and you will have your heart's desire. Rest my child!

Shalom, my precious daughter.

> [13] He who forms the mountains, creates the wind, and reveals His thoughts to man, He who turns dawn to darkness, and treads the high places of the earth; the LORD GOD Almighty is His name.
>
> Amos 4:13 NIV

As you can see from the preceding Scripture, GOD does reveal His thoughts to mankind and He will brush our hair with His wind as He longs to be close to us.

It is truly worth your time and submission to just wait for the voice of GOD, and when you hear Him speak to you, you will realize that He seems familiar to you and remember that whatever you hear, please discern if it is from GOD or the devil.

Not convinced that you can hear from GOD?

> ³ "Give ear and come to me; hear me that your soul may live. I will make an everlasting covenant with you, my faithful love promised to David.
> ⁴ See I have made him a witness to the peoples, a leader and commander of the peoples.
> ⁵ Surely you will summon nations you know not, and nations that do not know you will hasten to you, because of the LORD your GOD, the Holy One of Israel, for He has endowed you with splendor."
> ⁶ Seek the LORD while He may be found; call on Him while He is near.
> ⁷ Let the wicked forsake his way and the evil man his thoughts. Let him turn to the LORD, and He will have mercy on him, and to our GOD, for He will freely pardon.
> ⁸ "For my thoughts are not your thoughts, neither are your ways my ways," declares the LORD.
> ⁹ "As the heavens are higher than the earth; so are my ways higher than your ways, and my thoughts than your thoughts."
>
> Isaiah 55:3-9 NIV

GOD will speak to us and give us His thoughts, just as He promises in verse 3 above.

He never sleeps or slumbers, but His eyes are everywhere, all at once.

Unfortunately, however, we must be careful because the devil will put thoughts into our heads and confuse us if we are not well versed in hearing the voice of GOD.

I finally realized that if the thoughts I heard do not line up with what the Word of GOD says in the Bible, then I have once again been misled by Satan.

Believe me, it can happen and we must be always alert and aware of motives, either our own desires that could easily cause us to stumble, or motives that have been planted in our thoughts by others.

The devil is very clever and can deceive even the Holy Ones of GOD, which is why we are warned so many times in the Bible to watch and pray.

> ⁷ Dear children, do not let anyone lead you astray. He who does what is right is righteous, just as He is righteous.
> ⁸ He who does what is sinful is of the devil, because the devil has been sinning from the beginning. The reason the Son of GOD appeared was to destroy the devil's work.
> ⁹ No one who is born of GOD will continue to sin, because GOD's seed remains in him; he cannot go on sinning, because he has been born of GOD.
> ¹⁰ This is how we know who the children of GOD are and who the children of the devil are: anyone who does not do what is right is not a child of GOD; nor is anyone who does not love his brother.
>
> 1 John 3:7-10 NIV

The Bible rightly warns us about our tongues and the power of it.

With our tongue we can bless and curse and this is not to be done. Also, we must be careful what we speak because the devil is always roaring around, seeking who he can destroy. If you are always talking, the devil is listening, as well as GOD. He can use your words to place thoughts in your mind to attempt to deceive you into walking the way you wish, and not the way GOD desires for you.

Many do not realize the power of their words and the destruction they can set into motion in their own lives by speaking negative over their situations and their lives.

Taming the Tongue.
> ¹ Not many of you should presume to be teachers, my brothers, because you know that we who teach will be judged more strictly.
> ² We all stumble in many ways. If anyone is never at fault in what he says, he is a perfect man, able to keep his whole body in check.

³ When we put bits into the mouths of horses to make them obey us, we can turn the whole animal.
⁴ Or take ships as an example. Although they are so large and are driven by strong winds, they are steered by a very small rudder wherever the pilot wants to go.
⁵ Likewise the tongue is a small part of the body, but it makes great boasts. Consider what a great forest is set on fire by a small spark.
⁶ The tongue also is a fire, a world of evil among the parts of the body. It corrupts the whole person, sets the whole course of his life on fire, and is itself set on fire by hell.
⁷ All kinds of animals, birds, reptiles and creatures of the sea are being tamed and have been tamed by man,
⁸ but no man can tame the tongue. It is a restless evil, full of deadly poison.
⁹ With the tongue we praise our Lord and Father, and with it we curse men, who have been made in GOD's likeness.
¹⁰ Out of the same mouth come praise and cursing. My brothers, this should not be.
¹¹ Can both fresh water and salt water flow from the same spring?
¹² My brothers, can a fig tree bear olives, or a grapevine bear figs? Neither can a salt spring produce fresh water.

James 3:1-12 NIV

So, if we want to seek GOD, we must be conscious that when we pray and ask Him for blessings, we must be sure that we are not creating negative forces in our own lives by not controlling our tongues.

Another important lesson to learn is we must also be very aware of our thought life and not let the negative rule our minds. It will affect every area of our lives, either for blessings or cursings.

Therefore be careful how you live your lives, so you can enjoy yours to the fullest!

²² Flee the evil desires of youth, and pursue righteousness, faith, love and peace, along with those who call on the Lord out of a pure heart.

> [23] Don't have anything to do with foolish and stupid arguments, because you know they produce quarrels.
> [24] And the Lord's servant must not quarrel; instead, he must be kind to everyone, able to teach, not resentful.
> [25] Those who oppose him He must gently instruct, in the hope that GOD will grant them repentance leading them to knowledge of the truth,
> [26] and that they will come to their senses and escape from the trap of the devil, who has taken them captive to do his will.
>
> 2 Timothy 2:22-26 NIV

> [3] For though we live in the world, we do not wage war as the world does.
> [4] The weapons we fight with are not the weapons of the world. On the contrary, they have divine power to demolish strongholds.
> [5] We demolish arguments and every pretension that sets itself up against the knowledge of GOD, and we take captive every thought to make it obedient to Christ.
>
> 2 Corinthians 10:3-5 NIV

This is so important; we must take every thought captive and prove it up with the Word of GOD, especially in the beginning of our walk with the Lord.

GOD's way will always bring about peace in your heart and if you feel apprehension, take the next steps with caution, because GOD is a GOD of order and peace. So pray before your decisions and wait upon GOD to give you the answers to the questions you are seeking.

It may seem strange at first, but one day you will realize that you have involved GOD in every area of your life, and that makes all the difference in the turning pages of your world.

Just as when you start a new relationship, it is always that excitement and newness in the beginning that keeps us seeking. We want to discover the many new things about our new friendship and it is the same with GOD! He is longsuffering and waiting for you to discover the many things He wants to share with you!

This is an exciting adventure to travel and I encourage you to get started today!

Having a relationship with GOD is the most exciting adventure of life!

He will surprise you in ways you never thought, and He is not a dull and uninteresting person! He has humor, as a matter of fact; He created it, along with a very "alive" personality.

Walking with GOD is not boring at all, you don't give up anything, but you gain so much more in life, you will be amazed. He will show you life in ways you can only dream about!

Take a walk with Him and Quietly, He will speak to You.

In the early Church, Jesus walked among the people and He was, as we are, suffering and being tempted in every way. The difference is, as the Bible tells us, Jesus Christ never sinned!

Jesus was perfect in every way.

> [24] but because Jesus lives forever, He has a permanent priesthood.
> [25] Therefore He is able to save completely those who come to GOD through Him, because He always lives to intercede for them.
> [26] Such a high priest meets our need, one who is holy, blameless, pure, set apart from sinners, exalted above the Heavens.
> [27] Unlike the other high priests, He does not need to offer sacrifices day after day, first for His own sins, and then for the sins of the people. He sacrificed for their sins once for all when He offered Himself.
> [28] For the law appoints as high priests men who are weak; but the oath, which came after the law, appointed the Son, who has been made perfect forever.
>
> Hebrews 7:24-28 NIV

Once Jesus was crucified and ascended into Heaven, the Holy Spirit was then sent to the earth to the body of believers.

The Holy Spirit is alive and well today and He is interceding for us, just as our Lord Jesus is, and He is speaking to His people, His sheep that are called according to His divine purposes.

We who have given our lives to Jesus Christ are called "His sheep."

Just as in the day when Jesus walked with His disciples, the Holy Spirit comforted Jesus Christ, but not His disciples. The disciples had no need of the Holy Spirit, because they walked and talked with Jesus Himself, in the flesh. The Holy Spirit spoke only what the Father GOD told Him, and this same Holy Spirit now dwells in all believers and is speaking to us what the Father GOD is telling Him.

Jesus Promises the Holy Spirit.

[15] "If you love me, you will obey what I command.
[16] And I will ask the Father, and He will give you another Counselor to be with you forever;
[17] The Spirit of truth. The world cannot accept Him, because it neither sees Him, nor knows Him. But you know Him, for He lives with you and will be in you.
[18] I will not leave you as orphans; I will come to you.
[19] Before long, the world will not see me anymore, but you will see me. Because I live, you also will live.
[20] On that day you will realize that I am in my Father, and you are in me, and I am in you.
[21] Whoever has my commands and obeys them, he is the one who loves me. He who loves me will be loved by my Father, and I too will love him and show myself to him."

John 14:15-21 NIV

There are no surprises with GOD, once you reach this level of communicating with Him. There is much excitement and when you realize the closeness of His very breath near you, you will be amazed at His gentleness and kindness.

GOD's love for you is real and something to be sought after.

His message is still the same as in the days of the Old Testament, but we are closer now to the "beginning of the end" than at any other time in history.

Think of this word "history".....is it saying "His Story"?

March 1, 2005
4:00 a.m.

Your obedience is pleasing to me. Continue in me, you will be greatly rewarded. Do not quench the Holy Spirit; keep putting me first and not the things of this earth.

Be patient and wait upon me. All things will be accomplished in it's due season, just as the sun rises in the time I have set for it, you also will rise and shine at my appointed time, do not grow weary in waiting.

My eyes are upon you. I will guide your steps, walk in the way I have put before you, do not look to the left or the right. Keep your focus on me and see what mighty things I will do in your life, my hand is upon you.

I will cause even your enemies to honor you. I will put you in a high place of dwelling to teach the people what I have written so long ago. They ignore me; they do not know I am coming!

Tell the people I am not slack as some understand slackness.

I will not delay one minute past the appointed time. All must be accomplished as I've set in time, and although the times are perilous just wait to see it grow worse.

But my hand will be on my anointed ones and though fear, pestilence and suffering as in the days of Pharaoh, you will not be harmed!

My holy ones will be a beacon of light and there is much pruning to do in the Church before my return. The Church needs to wake up and not slumber! I am returning for my bride. Keep these words in your heart and ponder on them.

See how the darkness increases, but see how my glorious ones shine forth!

You will know the voices of truth on TBN, not all are called by me. Do not listen to strange teachings, but the grounded Word of GOD.

I do not change like the winds. I am the same, but my Spirit will show greater moves to strengthen my body before my return.

The Church is weak and not ready! If I walked among many today they would reject me, just as you feel rejected by some. This is as it should be; you are not of the world.

Keep shining your light before me so they see your good deeds and heart. Many will misunderstand, but do not loose heart, I am with you and I will not forsake you.

Shalom.

Just as any good parent prepares their child or children for each new day, GOD will prepare our days and counsel with us, if we will seek Him. GOD does not want us to live a defeated life and He wants us to let go of our defeated yesterdays.

The life that GOD intended for us to live was first of all, peaceful, loving and full of purpose.

Life was not meant to be so self-absorbed, filled with the apprehensions and disappointments of our lives. We were created to need each other and to be a servant to each other. We should be willing to lay down our lives for each other and not think of ourselves so highly.

Life Through the Spirit.
> [1] Therefore, there is now no condemnation for those who are in Christ Jesus,
> [2] because through Christ Jesus the law of the Spirit of life set me free from the law of sin and death.
> [3] For what the law was powerless to do in that it was weakened by the sinful nature, GOD did by sending His own Son in the likeness of sinful man to be a sin offering. And so He condemned sin in sinful man,
> [4] in order that the righteous requirements of the law might be fully met in us, who do not live according to the sinful nature but according to the Spirit.
> [5] Those who live according to the sinful nature have their minds set on what that nature desires; but those who live in accordance with the Spirit have their minds set on what the Spirit desires.
> [6] The mind of sinful man is death, but the mind controlled by the Spirit is life and peace;

⁷ the sinful mind is hostile to GOD. It does not submit to GOD's law, nor can it do so.

⁸ Those controlled by the sinful nature cannot please GOD.

⁹ You, however, are controlled not by the sinful nature but by the Spirit, if the Spirit of GOD lives in you. And if anyone does not have the Spirit of Christ, he does not belong to Christ.

¹⁰ But if Christ is in you, your body is dead because of sin, yet your spirit is alive because of righteousness.

¹¹ And if the Spirit of Him who raised Jesus from the dead is living in you, He who raised Christ from the dead will also give life to your mortal bodies through His Spirit, who lives in you.

¹² Therefore, brothers, we have an obligation, but it is not to the sinful nature, to live according to it.

¹³ For if you live according to the sinful nature, you will die; but if by the Spirit you put to death the misdeeds of the body, you will live;

¹⁴ Because those who are led by the Spirit of GOD are sons of GOD.

¹⁵ For you did not receive a Spirit that makes you a slave again to fear, but you received the Spirit of Sonship. And by Him we cry, "Abba, Father."

¹⁶ The Spirit himself testifies with our spirit that we are GOD's children.

¹⁷ Now if we are children, then we are heirs, heirs of GOD and co-heirs with Christ, if indeed we share in His sufferings in order that we may also share in His glory.

¹⁸ I consider that our present sufferings are not worth comparing with the glory that will be revealed in us.

¹⁹ The creation waits in eager expectation for the sons of GOD to be revealed.

²⁰ For the creation was subjected to frustration, not by its own choice, but by the will of the one who subjected it, in hope;

²¹ That the creation itself will be liberated from its bondage to decay and brought into the glorious freedom of the children of GOD.

²² We know that the whole creation has been groaning as in the pains of childbirth right up to the present time.

²³ Not only so, but we ourselves, who have the first-fruits of the Spirit, groan inwardly as we wait eagerly for our adoption as Sons, the redemption of our bodies.

²⁴ For in this hope we were saved. But hope that is seen is no hope at all. Who hopes for what he already has?

²⁵ But if we hope for what we do not yet have, we wait for it patiently.

²⁶ In the same way, the Spirit helps us in our weakness. We do not know what we ought to pray for, but the Spirit himself intercedes for us with groans that words cannot express.

²⁷ And He who searches our hearts knows the mind of the Spirit, because the Spirit intercedes for the Saints in accordance with GOD's will.

²⁸ And we know that in all things GOD works for the good of those who love Him, who have been called according to His purpose.

²⁹ For those GOD foreknew He also predestined to be conformed to the likeness of His Son, that He might be the firstborn among many brothers.

³⁰ And those He predestined, He also called; those He called, He also justified; those He justified, He also glorified.

³¹ What, then, shall we say in response to this? If GOD is for us, who can be against us?

³² He who did not spare His own Son, but gave Him up for us all, how will He not also, along with Him, graciously give us all things?

³³ Who will bring any charge against those whom GOD has chosen? It is GOD who justifies.

³⁴ Who is He that condemns? Christ Jesus, who died, more than that, who was raised to life, is at the right hand of GOD and is also interceding for us.

³⁵ Who shall separate us from the love of Christ? Shall trouble or hardship or persecution or famine or nakedness or danger or sword?

³⁶ As it is written: "For your sake we face death all day long; we are considered as sheep to be slaughtered."

[37] No, in all these things we are more than conquerors through Him who loved us.
[38] For I am convinced that neither death nor life, neither angels nor demons, neither the present nor the future, nor any powers,
[39] neither height nor depth, nor anything else in all creation, will be able to separate us from the love of GOD that is in Christ Jesus our Lord.

Romans 8 NIV

I am so comforted by the preceding chapter and the promises of GOD that He graciously reminds us of our importance to Him.

Jesus Christ will always be our Rock, our Healer, our Protector, our Guide and our All in All, if only we will open up our hearts to accept Him. I hope and pray that He is everything to you in your life!

Jesus Christ is no respecter of persons and He will love you in the same way, each and every day of your life.

GOD's character is beyond reproach.

He has granted life to us for the living and He has given each of us a "free will" to live as we choose. His love is so great that He will not force Himself on anyone; He will let us all make our choices in life. When we choose to live outside of the Will of GOD, our lives will reflect that choice.

Living in GOD's perfect will for us takes a lot of surrender of self, inner-reflection and time spent praying and reading of His Word, His Holy Bible.

GOD will not give us a burden that we are not equipped to carry.

Just as if you are not comfortable going to some far off and distant poverty stricken country as a missionary, I assure you, GOD will not send you into that situation.

He knows your hearts desire, He is the one that placed those desires in each of us. He will send you in the way you would be willing to walk and He will equip you, because He loves you.

Jesus loves you so much that He chose to take your sins upon Himself and to die for YOU!

Chapter Two

Radical Thinking?

If there is one mission in this book, it is this, to open our eyes to see Jesus Christ, "Yeshua" who walked this earth before us and changed the course of history.

I don't simply want our hearts affected, I want our hearts changed!

I want you to know beyond a "shadow of a doubt" that Jesus loves You.

Jesus did not call the perfect into His family; He called the sinners, the lost, the strung out on life, and the down and out people. He lived daily with the downcast of society. He healed them, and restored them to wholeness in every area of their lives. He cast out demons from them; He fed and taught them the true value of life. He also taught the Rulers, the Kings and the rich people of that society, none was left out of Jesus' teachings, and His love for them.

Jesus never exalted Himself before mankind, He was their Servant.

The Church today has a mission and a calling to tell the world the good news of His perfect love. We are called to be a light to those living in the darkness!

So, where are those who are calling forth a higher purpose in each of us?

By and large it seems the Church is failing in their approaches to teach and show the love of Jesus Christ and His examples for living.

A lot of Churches are teaching a word of compromise and apathy, not wanting to rock the boat of society and allowing society to dictate their lifestyles to us.

I am blessed to have found a wonderful Christian Publisher for this book. I've discovered that some "Christian" Publishers won't publish a book like this one, if it has any "deep" truth to it and would cause any controversy. This is so sad to me that they are more interested in profits, than souls saved and the truth taught.

Jesus Christ was a man of controversy! Jesus warns us that the world hated Him and would also hate His Saints.

The World Hates the Disciples.

> 18 "If the world hates you, keep in mind that it hated me first.
> 19 If you belonged to the world, it would love you as its own. As it is, you do not belong to the world, but I have chosen you out of the world. That is why the world hates you.
> 20 Remember the words I spoke to you: 'No servant is greater than his master.' If they persecuted me, they will persecute you also. If they obeyed my teaching, they will obey yours also.
> 21 They will treat you this way because of my name, for they do not know the One who sent me.
> 22 If I had not come and spoken to them, they would not be guilty of sin. Now, however, they have no excuse for their sin.
> 23 He who hates me hates my Father as well.
> 24 If I had not done among them what no one else did, they would not be guilty of sin. But now they have seen these miracles, and yet they have hated both me and my Father.
> 25 But this is to fulfill what is written in their Law: 'They hated me without reason.'"
>
> John 15:18-25 NIV

The gift giver, the life changer and the world hated Him.

What quiet desperation He must have felt walking up that road to His destiny, knowing that only a few would truly love Him with all their heart and soul and He would suffer to the point of sweating blood.

Do we really deserve the love of Jesus Christ?

What about the healings, the miracles that Jesus Christ still performs today in so many lives?

I know in my own life, He has graciously healed me many times. He cast out demons from my soul that had dictated my life for 43 years.

He restored my life and He is still the same today as He was at the beginning of time. He is no respecter of persons and He will heal you and set you free from your bondages!

Jesus taught us that the miracles He performed, His Disciples would be equipped to perform and even greater miracles we would do than Jesus himself.

How, you ask?

His Disciples are filled with the same Holy Spirit that abided in Jesus Christ, sent down from the throne of GOD in Heaven, to equip us to do a mighty work before He returns.

> [11] "Believe me when I say that I am in the Father and the Father is in me; or at least believe on the evidence of the miracles themselves.
> [12] I tell you the truth, anyone who has faith in me will do what I have been doing. He will do even greater things than these, because I am going to the Father.
> [13] And I will do whatever you ask in my name, so that the Son may bring glory to the Father.
> [14] You may ask me for anything in my name, and I will do it.
> [15] If you love me, you will obey what I command."
>
> John 14:11-15 NIV

Because of Jesus' sacrifice on the cross, He paid the price for our sin and He made a provision for us to be cleansed from all unrighteousness. I don't believe any of us deserve His love! He loves us and when you give your heart to Jesus Christ, you will never be the same and you will experience His unconditional love for You.

In saying this, I will preface the next sentence by telling you that there are Churches who are allowing sinful lives and lifestyles to be a part of the ministry; thereby giving the idea to people that this way of life is acceptable to GOD. They preach that GOD is purely love and there are no consequences for their choices.

This is not the truth, but a spin on the teachings of the devil!

The devil wants you to fall into deep deception and not know the GOD who created us.

GOD is just, righteous and holy! He cannot dwell in the darkness, but by the light, He illuminates the truth to those who seek Him.

GOD wants us to live a life "full of love" and "acceptance" of people, but not to live in "sin" or to love the sin, but we must love the sinner!

We are to open the eyes of the people and to tell them the truth, so that their eternal destination is one with GOD, not one with the devil.

[9] Love must be sincere. Hate what is evil; cling to what is good.
[10] Be devoted to one another in brotherly love. Honor one another above yourselves.
[11] Never be lacking in zeal, but keep your spiritual fervor, serving the Lord.
[12] Be joyful in hope, patient in affliction, faithful in prayer.
[13] Share with GOD's people who are in need. Practice hospitality.
[14] Bless those who persecute you; bless and do not curse.
[15] Rejoice with those who rejoice; mourn with those who mourn.
[16] Live in harmony with one another. Do not be proud, but be willing to associate with people of low position. Do not be conceited.
[17] Do not repay anyone evil for evil. Be careful to do what is right in the eyes of everybody.
[18] If it is possible, as far as it depends on you, live at peace with everyone.
[19] Do not take revenge, my friends, but leave room for GOD's wrath, for it is written: "It is mine to avenge; I will repay," says the Lord.

> [20] On the contrary: "If your enemy is hungry, feed him; if he is thirsty, give him something to drink. In doing this, you will heap burning coals on his head."
> [21] Do not be overcome by evil, but overcome evil with good.
> Romans 12:9-21 NIV

His creation, we are the ones that were created in His image, and we were not meant to ever live one minute, let alone an eternity, in a place called Hell. It is real and billions will find their lost souls dwelling there for all of eternity.

The Day of the Lord.

> [1] Dear friends, this is now my second letter to you. I have written both of them as reminders to stimulate you to wholesome thinking.
> [2] I want you to recall the words spoken in the past by the holy prophets and the command given by our Lord and Savior through your apostles.
> [3] First of all, you must understand that in the last days scoffers will come, scoffing and following their own evil desires.
> [4] They will say, "Where is this 'coming' He promised? Ever since our fathers died, everything goes on as it has since the beginning of creation."
> [5] But they deliberately forget that long ago by GOD's word the heavens existed and the earth was formed out of water and by water.
> [6] By these waters also the world of that time was deluged and destroyed.
> [7] By the same word the present heavens and earth are reserved for fire, being kept for the Day of Judgment and destruction of ungodly men.
> [8] But do not forget this one thing, dear friends: With the Lord a day is like a thousand years, and a thousand years are like a day.
> [9] The Lord is not slow in keeping His promise, as some understand slowness. He is patient with you, not wanting anyone to perish, but everyone to come to repentance.

10 But the day of the Lord will come like a thief. The heavens will disappear with a roar; the elements will be destroyed by fire, and the earth and everything in it will be laid bare.

11 Since everything will be destroyed in this way, what kind of people ought you to be? You ought to live holy and Godly lives;

12 as you look forward to the day of GOD and speed its coming. That day will bring about the destruction of the heavens by fire, and the elements will melt in the heat.

13 But in keeping with His promise we are looking forward to a new heaven and a new earth, the home of righteousness.

14 So then, dear friends, since you are looking forward to this, make every effort to be found spotless, blameless and at peace with Him.

15 Bear in mind that our Lord's patience means salvation, just as our dear brother Paul also wrote you with the wisdom that GOD gave him.

16 He writes the same way in all his letters, speaking in them of these matters. His letters contain some things that are hard to understand, which ignorant and unstable people distort, as they do the other Scriptures, to their own destruction.

17 Therefore, dear friends, since you already know this, be on your guard so that you may not be carried away by the error of lawless men and fall from your secure position.

18 But grow in the grace and knowledge of our Lord and Savior Jesus Christ. To him be glory both now and forever! Amen.

2 Peter 3 NIV

Are you seeking for the Lord's sudden return?

Quietly, HE speaks; are you listening and longing for Jesus Christ?

I belong to a dynamic, spirit-filled Church and I see the conduct of a few that are not living a fruit-filled life for Jesus. It is the same with any Church you attend, because none of us are perfect. I am not speaking out of turn, but simply saying that many people are not walking as if their life has any impact, any meaning, and they have little joy in their lives!

If this is the life of some believers, we must realize that it is even worse in the world, where GOD is not known in the people's hearts.

Do you accept that GOD loves you?

GOD knows our hearts, our minds and our motives. I remind myself of His teachings so that I do not fall into temptation and take for granted the calling and the gifts He has given me.

GOD's love is bountiful in mercy and grace and I do not take this lightly!

I myself have been forgiven from a very sin-filled life and I strive to now live a life of holiness, always watching to be careful of what I watch and listen to.

I was not raised in a Christian home and I did not know the love or the life of Jesus Christ. My parents taught me to be good, honest and to treat people the way that I would want to be treated. That, in itself, is a good teaching, but it would not have prevented my spirit from going to Hell for all eternity.

It also didn't keep me from drinking, taking drugs and being promiscuous after my first divorce. I suffered through many trials since then, before I came to Jesus and He forgave me and cleansed me from my wicked life and showed me a better way to live.

I am so very thankful for His love, His mercy and grace!

He forgave me and He will forgive you too!

Many good parents are teaching their children these same "golden rules," but they are not teaching them about Jesus and to cast off the sin in their lives.

You cannot lead someone to Jesus Christ, if you don't know the way, and sadly many do not know the way, the truth and the life of Him who loves them so much, that He died for them.

Jesus died for all of us and the entire world needs Him as their Savior.

If we have invited Jesus Christ into our hearts, we must be careful what we allow into our eyes, ears and hearts, so we don't defile the temple of GOD, which is our living body.

If you haven't accepted Jesus Christ as your Savior, then your body is being used for your pleasure and not for GOD's.

In order to walk in victory in every area of our lives, we must live for Jesus Christ and be totally aware that we are living in a spiritual battle! We cannot afford to be slack in protecting our spirit and soul.

Right now there is a battle going on for your spirit.

I'm not suggesting that even if you walk a perfect walk with GOD, that you won't have problems, because you will.

We read about the life of Job in the Bible and see that through all his sufferings, he did not curse GOD and die like his wife wanted him to. Because of the character of Job, GOD restored his health, and returned to Job twice what He previously allowed Satan to take from him.

Job's Second Test.

> [1] On another day the Angels came to present themselves before the LORD, and Satan also came with them to present himself before Him.
> [2] And the LORD said to Satan, "Where have you come from?" Satan answered the LORD, "From roaming through the earth and going back and forth in it."
> [3] Then the LORD said to Satan, "Have you considered my servant Job? There is no one on earth like him; he is blameless and upright, a man who fears GOD and shuns evil. And he still maintains his integrity, though you incited me against him to ruin him without any reason."
> [4] "Skin for skin!" Satan replied. "A man will give all he has for his own life;
> [5] but stretch out your hand and strike his flesh and bones, and he will surely curse you to your face."
> [6] The LORD said to Satan, "Very well, then, he is in your hands; but you must spare his life."
> [7] So Satan went out from the presence of the LORD and afflicted Job with painful sores from the soles of his feet to the top of his head.
> [8] Then Job took a piece of broken pottery and scraped himself with it as he sat among the ashes.
> [9] His wife said to him, "Are you still holding on to your integrity? Curse GOD and die!"

¹⁰ He replied, "You are talking like a foolish woman. Shall we accept good from GOD, and not trouble?" In all this, Job did not sin in what he said.

Job's Three Friends.

¹¹ When Job's three friends, Eliphaz the Temanite, Bildad the Shuhite and Zophar the Naamathite, heard about all the troubles that had come upon him, they set out from their homes and met together by agreement to go and sympathize with him and comfort him.
¹² When they saw him from a distance, they could hardly recognize him; they began to weep aloud, and they tore their robes and sprinkled dust on their heads.
¹³ Then they sat on the ground with him for seven days and seven nights. No one said a word to him, because they saw how great his suffering was.

Job 2 NIV

Many times in our own lives, GOD will put us through tests to try our faith and to grow us and refine us. I have been through too many to even count and I am thankful for the testing, it has made me stronger.

So, even though I am trying to convince you to give your heart to Jesus Christ, I still must also say that life is full of obstacles, trials and temptations!

I am also saying that with Jesus as your Savior, you will not be walking alone and Jesus will equip you for all the trials and temptations in your life. He does protect His own and He will keep you under His mighty wings of love.

Another point I want to make in this chapter of "Radical Thinking" is this: some professing to be "Christians" watch "R" rated television shows, and movies, just as those who don't profess to belong to Jesus Christ. Consequently, these Christians have no power in their walk with GOD and they struggle with sin in their life. They have polluted their bodies with "sin" and so often wonder why their lives are so unfulfilling.

Do you know anyone like this? Perhaps they have kept you from seeking GOD in your own life.

You see them lament over their life and they often question, "What has gone wrong?" They falsely believe they are serving GOD, yet they partake in entertainment that Jesus would be offended with.

Let's look at it this way. Remember the "Leave it to Beaver" days when things were simple, and you might say, boring? People were expected to act and treat people a certain way. We were kind to our elders and we gave them the respect the Bible instructs us to.

We wore a different kind of clothing; we said "please" and "thank you" more often. We didn't hear cursing flowing out of people's mouths in public. Well, if you are over the age of 30, you get the idea.

Now, for instance, you start watching a show with an "R" rating, and the language, dress, violence and sex will, at first, be shocking, yet a bit thrilling to watch. It might be kind of like doing something you feel you really shouldn't be doing, but you are enticed by the temptation.

Now, let's say that you continue watching about five or six programs, pretty soon you are de-sensitized and it no longer bother's you and you half expect the language, the dress, the violence and the sex. You watch the programming now to get a thrill and an escape from reality.

Now, go back and watch the "Leave it to Beaver" show. You won't be able to stand it, there is no thrill and you are bored.

Am I right?

Maybe you believe the "R" rated show isn't so bad, but can you see by my example above, that before long it will take more and more "risky" television for your appetite to be satisfied?

This is the same with "sin" and how it gets in our lives. Little by little, we let down our guard and we get casual and then the devil has a foot-hold in our lives!

What was once just good old entertainment, you won't want to give the time of day to, and we are living in just such a world!

Children have seen so much by the time they are in elementary school, which our parents didn't see or expose us to. Pornography, violence and hatred have slowly slipped up on our society over a matter of years and many people are no longer shocked by it.

> [17] So I tell you this, and insist on it in the Lord, that you must no longer live as the Gentiles do, in the futility of their thinking.
> [18] They are darkened in their understanding and separated from the life of GOD because of the ignorance that is in them due to the hardening of their hearts.
> [19] Having lost all sensitivity, they have given themselves over to sensuality so as to indulge in every kind of impurity, with a continual lust for more.
> [20] You, however, did not come to know Christ that way.
> [21] Surely you heard of Him and were taught in Him in accordance with the truth that is in Jesus.
> [22] You were taught, with regard to your former way of life, to put off your old self, which is being corrupted by its deceitful desires;
> [23] to be made new in the attitude of your minds;
> [24] and to put on the new self; created to be like GOD in true righteousness and holiness.
> [25] Therefore each of you must put off falsehood and speak truthfully to His neighbor, for we are all members of one body.
> [26] "In your anger do not sin:" Do not let the sun go down while you are still angry,
> [27] and do not give the devil a foothold.
> [28] He who has been stealing must steal no longer, but must work, doing something useful with his own hands, that he may have something to share with those in need.
> [29] Do not let any unwholesome talk come out of your mouths, but only what is helpful for building others up according to their needs, that it may benefit those who listen.
> [30] And do not grieve the Holy Spirit of GOD, with whom you were sealed for the day of redemption.
> [31] Get rid of all bitterness, rage and anger, brawling and slander, along with every form of malice.

³² Be kind and compassionate to one another, forgiving each other, just as in Christ GOD forgave you.

Ephesians 4:17-32 NIV

Remember above, where I remarked that maybe "R" rated movies and television shows might not be considered bad to you?

Let's read the message below and glean from the heart of GOD, His thoughts.

June 26, 2005
4:45 a.m.

My beloved,

Do not be anxious about you and Jessica's future, but trust in me and let me lead you step by step. Walking in faith means you trust where I am leading you and it also keeps you from anxious thoughts. Remember I am with you both and I love you.

You both have a calling on your life and the men I bring to you will also be preachers of the gospel. You will be equally yoked with them and do not go by what things look like in the natural, I am the GOD of the Supernatural and I have your futures in my mighty hand.

I do not change like the shifting winds; I am a GOD of order and not confusion or chaos. You keep abiding in my WORD and keep seeking me.

Take time to read my WORD and to sit quietly before me, I can do much work in your hearts. Remember that you are to represent me wherever you go and that people are watching your attitudes and they hope to see you trip up and not walk out your faith according to my words.

Be patient with yourselves and each other. You are both on the Potter's wheel and I am reshaping and molding you both by the things you suffer. You are to live in accordance to your calling and to represent my Son, Jesus in everything you do.

The world needs to wake up and not be in slumber about the evil all around them.

Remember to keep your eye gates pure and to guard what you see on television. Satan uses this device to blind the multitudes and to keep them wanting more and more evil to entertain themselves. America is a most ungodly nation and one I have blessed abundantly.

If it were not for my holy elect, I would completely take my hand of protection from her and let Satan destroy it.

My Church is to be a light and it should be dispelling the darkness. Many do not walk in the light; their lamps have grown dim because of the sin in their lives.

My holy ones need to purify their hearts, cleanse their minds of the evil they see and look to me, the author and perfector of their faith. Without me there is no reason to live holy and upright lives. Your lives would be for nothing, but to satisfy your earthly, fleshy desires.

Keep heeding my voice and my leading. Keep sowing the books to those I tell you. You will reap a great harvest and the souls of the lost saved will be jewels in your crown.

My WORD never returns void and it will accomplish much. Keep spreading the good news and my gospel in simple form. People are dying all around you without their sins being forgiven. Each time a soul dies without my forgiveness, they go to the deep and it is another stripe on my Son's back, He suffers much watching the multitudes. If only more could have the heart of Jesus, if only more could understand that this is what their lives are all about.

You have been given an opportunity to share this good news with many who live as your neighbors. Share my gospel with them and do not worry about what others may think of you. Remember you are handing them a life preserver to a drowning person. Many will never walk into my holy assemblies of Church, they are filled with shame and guilt, and you must bring it to them, where they live and work.

You start to witness to others and watch the blessings flow over into your life.

Write up a tract if you wish to aid you. Remember all you have to do is open your mouth and the Holy Spirit will give you the words, you do not need to be afraid, you are my mighty servant in whom I have equipped to go into all the world. Start right where you are at.

Shalom, my precious child.

I hope you know by reading the above that GOD does not want us to live our life's watching this type of entertainment that the majority of our society exalts and hungers for. It is a weapon the enemy uses to get us off track and to consider not ourselves as being instruments of GOD's peace and love.

GOD requires us to live a righteous and holy life! Is this "Radical" thinking to you?

Perhaps it is for some, but then it is the classic tale of good versus evil. It has been that way since the beginning of time.

Let's look back at the beginning.

In the book of Genesis, Adam and Eve fell out of GOD's plan for their life and they were cast out of the Garden of Eden.

The Fall of Man.

> [1] Now the serpent was craftier than any of the wild animals the LORD GOD had made. He said to the woman, "Did GOD really say, 'You must not eat from any tree in the garden'?"
> [2] The woman said to the serpent, "We may eat fruit from the trees in the garden,"
> [3] but GOD did say, "You must not eat fruit from the tree that is in the middle of the garden, and you must not touch it, or you will die."
> [4] "You will not surely die," the serpent said to the woman.
> [5] "For GOD knows that when you eat of it your eyes will be opened, and you will be like GOD; knowing good and evil."
> [6] When the woman saw that the fruit of the tree was good for food and pleasing to the eye, and also desirable for gaining wisdom, she took some and ate it. She also gave some to her husband, who was with her, and he ate it.
> [7] Then the eyes of both of them were opened, and they realized they were naked; so they sewed fig leaves together and made coverings for themselves.
> [8] Then the man and his wife heard the sound of the LORD GOD as He was walking in the garden in the cool of the day, and they hid from the LORD GOD among the trees of the garden.
> [9] But the LORD GOD called to the man, "Where are you?"

10 He answered, "I heard you in the garden, and I was afraid because I was naked; so I hid."
11 And he said, "Who told you that you were naked? Have you eaten from the tree that I commanded you not to eat from?"
12 The man said, "The woman you put here with me, she gave me some fruit from the tree, and I ate it."
13 Then the LORD GOD said to the woman, "What is this you have done?" The woman said, "The serpent deceived me, and I ate."
14 So the LORD GOD said to the serpent, "Because you have done this, cursed are you above all the livestock and all the wild animals! You will crawl on your belly and you will eat dust all the days of your life."
15 "And I will put enmity between you and the woman, and between your offspring and hers; he will crush your head, and you will strike his heel."
16 To the woman He said, "I will greatly increase your pains in childbearing; with pain you will give birth to children. Your desire will be for your husband, and he will rule over you."
17 To Adam He said, "Because you listened to your wife and ate from the tree about which I commanded you, 'You must not eat of it,' Cursed is the ground because of you; through painful toil you will eat of it all the days of your life.
18 It will produce thorns and thistles for you and you will eat the plants of the field.
19 By the sweat of your brow you will eat your food until you return to the ground, since from it you were taken; for dust you are and to dust you will return."
20 Adam named his wife Eve, because she would become the mother of all the living.
21 The LORD GOD made garments of skin for Adam and his wife and clothed them.
22 And the LORD GOD said, "The man has now become like one of us, knowing good and evil. He must not be allowed to reach out his hand and take also from the tree of life and eat, and live forever."

> [23] So the LORD GOD banished him from the Garden of Eden to work the ground from which he had been taken.
> [24] After He drove the man out, He placed on the east side of the Garden of Eden cherubim and a flaming sword flashing back and forth to guard the way to the tree of life.
>
> Genesis 3 NIV

Consequently, as you've just read above, we are born into this world with a "sin" nature and to be right with GOD, we have to meet Jesus Christ at the foot of the cross (figuratively speaking) and repent of our sinful lifestyles.

Even if you never considered yourself a sinner, you were born a sinner, as a consequence of our ancestors, Adam and Eve.

So, if you have lost a son or daughter at a young and tender age, do not despair, GOD has your child in Heaven with Him. Our children are exempt from going to Hell, if they died before the age of accountability.

GOD does not expect our babies and our young children to understand His ways and therefore, they do not need to repent.

Once a child reaches the age of accountability, which I'm not exactly sure what age that represents, but I would guess around 12 or so, then they must repent of their sins and ask Jesus into their hearts to be saved.

However, as accountable adults, we must accept His love and forgiveness into our hearts and be changed from the inside out, if we want to live with GOD for all eternity in Heaven.

If we don't surrender our lives to Jesus Christ, we will spend our eternity in Hell.

It really is that simple!

Not making a decision to follow Jesus is making an eternal decision that cannot be changed after you have breathed your last breath. Think about your choices carefully, because you do not know what hour your life will end. You can't control that, but you can control your eternal destiny.

What will be your choice?

The world needs us to be willing to take a stand for righteousness, for purity of living, to bring back the morals our society desperately needs. Our world is so filled with tolerance that we don't call "sin" what it is anymore!

We must be willing to be a non-conformist, to be a Champion to our families and our world. We need to strive to listen to the voice of GOD, He is speaking!

Are you hearing what Jesus Christ is saying to the Churches? What about in your own life?

We justify the homosexual population as living their own way, they claim it is a life suited for them.

We justify the violence by blaming the entertainment community.

We justify our fallen values because of the rising divorce rate.

We justify the drugs, alcohol and every other destructive choice as just "a way of life," and "free-will" choices of being politically correct.

What we don't realize is that Satan has broken down our society in such a way that we can't see him destroying the world's population and deceiving millions of people!

That is why the Bible warns us about Satan and his demons. He is described as a roaring lion, seeking people to destroy.

> [8] Be self-controlled and alert. Your enemy the devil prowls around like a roaring lion looking for someone to devour.
> [9] Resist him, standing firm in the faith, because you know that your brothers throughout the world are undergoing the same kind of sufferings.
> [10] And the GOD of all grace, who called you to His eternal glory in Christ, after you have suffered a little while, will Himself restore you and make you strong, firm and steadfast.
> [11] To Him be the power for ever and ever. Amen.
>
> 1 Peter 5:8-11 NIV

If we want to have a better life, we have to make better choices!

Jesus Christ is a compassionate man, full of grace, mercy and total forgiveness!

Jesus Christ died on a cross, so those who accept Him into their hearts can live with Him in Heaven and have eternal life. He defeated death, once for all!

He was raised on the third day and He arose with power, and that same power dwells in every believer of Jesus Christ.

While living on the Earth, Jesus set an example for us to follow and His examples are illustrated throughout the entire Bible.

I like the acronym "Basic Instructions Before Leaving Earth." This is the total sum of what the Bible teaches.

It is invaluable to those who take the time to read it.

You will find GOD's answers to many of life's problems, it only takes a hungry heart and a searching to find the truth and the truth will set you free from the bondages of your life.

We will all leave this earth one day, when our body deteriorates and dies. It is important to know the journey your spirit takes, once it leaves your body.

Jesus Christ provides the way by which we can be saved from Hell, which is where your spirit will go, unless you have been saved from this destiny.

It starts with giving your life to Jesus Christ!

Don't live your life not accepting Christ because of your Christian neighbor or co-worker who you see has little or no joy in their life!

We cannot let the devil steal our gift of salvation by pointing our attention to those "church people" who don't live the way we expect Christians to live.

Society calls them hypocrites, I believe they are trying to seek the truth, but don't live the truth. There is a big difference!

Attending Church doesn't make us a Christian, not by any stretch of the imagination, nor does eating at McDonalds make us a hamburger. We see the examples of our choices in our bodies, and it is the same with our minds, our actions and our attitudes.

If we feed on what the world is teaching us and not what Jesus Christ is teaching us, our minds and attitudes will be filled with negative thoughts and actions. We will have little hope and only existing from the day to day.

Once we find Jesus Christ and accept Him as our Savior, then we will finally have the void in our heart filled and we will have a different outlook on life. Suddenly, your life will have meaning and a purpose and you will discover things you never knew.

Once you take this step, you should attend Church regularly and grow in the knowledge of Jesus Christ!

Church serves as a great source in keeping us uplifted and loved; however, it is not a substitute for GOD and it never will be. If you belong to a Spirit-filled Church, GOD will dwell among you and you will feel His presence as He surrounds you with wings of love.

GOD expects and calls us to fellowship with one another.

> [5] Therefore, when Christ came into the world, He said: "Sacrifice and offering you did not desire, but a body you prepared for me;
> [6] with burnt offerings and sin offerings you were not pleased.
> [7] Then I said, 'Here I am, it is written about me in the scroll, I have come to do your will, O GOD.'"
> [8] First He said, "Sacrifices and offerings, burnt offerings and sin offerings you did not desire, nor were you pleased with them" (although the law required them to be made).
> [9] Then He said, "Here I am, I have come to do your will." He sets aside the first to establish the second.
> [10] And by that will, we have been made holy through the sacrifice of the body of Jesus Christ once for all.
> [11] Day after day every priest stands and performs his religious duties; again and again he offers the same sacrifices, which can never take away sins.
> [12] But when this priest had offered for all time one sacrifice for sins, He sat down at the right hand of GOD.
> [13] Since that time He waits for His enemies to be made His footstool;
> [14] Because by one sacrifice He has made perfect forever those who are being made holy.
> [15] The Holy Spirit also testifies to us about this. First He says:
> [16] "This is the covenant I will make with them after that time," says the Lord. "I will put my laws in their hearts, and I will write them on their minds."
> [17] Then He adds: "Their sins and lawless acts I will remember no more."
> [18] And where these have been forgiven, there is no longer any sacrifice for sin.

¹⁹ Therefore, brothers, since we have confidence to enter the Most Holy Place by the blood of Jesus,

²⁰ by a new and living way opened for us through the curtain, that is, His body,

²¹ and since we have a great priest over the house of GOD,

²² let us draw near to GOD with a sincere heart in full assurance of faith, having our hearts sprinkled to cleanse us from a guilty conscience and having our bodies washed with pure water.

²³ Let us hold unswervingly to the hope we profess, for He who promised is faithful.

²⁴ And let us consider how we may spur one another on toward love and good deeds.

²⁵ Let us not give up meeting together, as some are in the habit of doing, but let us encourage one another, and all the more as you see the Day approaching.

²⁶ If we deliberately keep on sinning after we have received the knowledge of the truth, no sacrifice for sins is left;

²⁷ But only a fearful expectation of judgment and of raging fire that will consume the enemies of GOD.

²⁸ Anyone who rejected the Law of Moses died without mercy on the testimony of two or three witnesses.

²⁹ How much more severely do you think a man deserves to be punished who has trampled the Son of GOD under foot, who has treated as an unholy thing the blood of the covenant that sanctified him, and who has insulted the Spirit of grace?

³⁰ For we know Him who said, "It is mine to avenge; I will repay," and again, "The Lord will judge His people."

³¹ "It is a dreadful thing to fall into the hands of the living GOD."

³² Remember those earlier days after you had received the light, when you stood your ground in a great contest in the face of suffering?

³³ Sometimes you were publicly exposed to insult and persecution; at other times you stood side by side with those who were so treated.

³⁴ You sympathized with those in prison and joyfully accepted the confiscation of your property, because you knew that you yourselves had better and lasting possessions.

⁳⁵ So do not throw away your confidence; it will be richly rewarded.
³⁶ You need to persevere so that when you have done the will of GOD, you will receive what He has promised.
³⁷ For in just a very little while, He who is coming will come and will not delay.
³⁸ "But my righteous one will live by faith. And if he shrinks back, I will not be pleased with him."
³⁹ But we are not of those who shrink back and are destroyed, but of those who believe and are saved.

Hebrews 10:5-39 NIV

As you have read from the preceding Scriptures, we are to be instruments of His peace and His love!

Our Churches should be a safe place to lift each other up and encourage one other. We must keep our focus on Jesus Christ and not the imperfections of each other, and we will live a victorious life!

We must be careful not to judge each other, because by the same measurement we use to judge, it will be used to judge us, by the Lord.

¹ "Do not judge or you to will be judged.
² For in the same way you judge others, you will be judged, and with the measure you use, it will be measured to you."
³ "Why do you look at the speck of sawdust in your brother's eye and pay no attention to the plank in your own eye?
⁴ How can you say to your brother, 'Let me take the speck out of your eye,' when all the time there is a plank in your own eye?
⁵ You hypocrite, first take the plank out of your own eye, and then you will see clearly to remove the speck from your brother's eye."

Matthew 7:1-5 NIV

I often ask myself why we are so weak and immersed in our problems, that we don't help those around us. The answer is found in the following Scripture.

It reminds me that we are living in a real spiritual battle, day by day, and we can't see it, but we can feel the negative effects of it on our lives each day and in many ways.

GOD instructs us to put on the armor of GOD so that we can stand the trials of the devil.

> [10] Finally, be strong in the Lord and in His mighty power.
> [11] Put on the full armor of GOD so that you can take your stand against the devil's schemes.
> [12] For our struggle is not against flesh and blood, but against the rulers, against the authorities, against the powers of this dark world and against the spiritual forces of evil in the heavenly realms.
> [13] Therefore put on the full armor of GOD, so that when the day of evil comes, you may be able to stand your ground, and after you have done everything, to stand.
> [14] Stand firm then, with the belt of truth buckled around your waist, with the breastplate of righteousness in place;
> [15] And with your feet fitted with the readiness that comes from the gospel of peace.
> [16] In addition to all this, take up the shield of faith, with which you can extinguish all the flaming arrows of the evil one.
> [17] Take the helmet of salvation and the sword of the Spirit, which is the word of GOD.
> [18] And pray in the Spirit on all occasions with all kinds of prayers and requests. With this in mind, be alert and always keep on praying for all the Saints.
>
> Ephesians 6:10-18 NIV

Each day we encounter the negative filth of this world and it affects us, no matter how hard we try to not let it influence us.

That is why Jesus reminds us to renew our minds daily, by reading the Word of GOD. It cleanses our polluted temples and gives us a fresh perspective as we lay down our lives and our worries and remind ourselves of the goodness of Jesus Christ.

> ¹Therefore, I urge you, brothers, in view of GOD's mercy, to offer your bodies as living sacrifices, holy and pleasing to GOD, this is your spiritual act of worship.
> ²Do not conform any longer to the pattern of this world, but be transformed by the renewing of your mind. Then you will be able to test and approve what GOD's will is, His good, pleasing and perfect will.
> ³For by the grace given me I say to every one of you: Do not think of yourself more highly than you ought, but rather think of yourself with sober judgment, in accordance with the measure of faith GOD has given you.
> ⁴Just as each of us has one body with many members, and these members do not all have the same function;
> ⁵So in Christ we who are many form one body, and each member belongs to all the others.
> ⁶We have different gifts, according to the grace given us.
>
> Romans 12:1-6 NIV

The good news is we have a GOD who loves us and calls us to Him!

When we cast all our cares on Him, we will find Him most faithful to unload our burdens on and He will always supply all our needs.

It takes a few requirements however; and we must be willing to lay down our pride and our life's agenda, and seek GOD in everything we do.

We need to turn our lives over to Jesus Christ and surrender our own agenda's and become a part of the family of GOD, if we want to live our eternity in Heaven.

You do have a choice, your spirit can live for all eternity in Heaven or in Hell, and the choice is totally up to You!

If you do not accept Jesus Christ as your Savior, you will find your life much harder, and the burdens heavy to carry without depending on the Rock of Jesus to lift you up and carry you through life's storms.

Your spirit will also dwell for all eternity in a place called Hell, or the Lake of Fire, which was created and reserved for Satan and his demons.

The Dead Are Judged.

> [11] Then I saw a great white throne and Him who was seated on it. Earth and sky fled from His presence, and there was no place for them.
> [12] And I saw the dead, great and small, standing before the throne, and books were opened. Another book was opened, which is the Book of Life. The dead were judged according to what they had done as recorded in the books.
> [13] The sea gave up the dead that were in it, and death and Hades gave up the dead that were in them, and each person was judged according to what he had done.
> [14] Then death and Hades were thrown into the Lake of Fire. The Lake of Fire is the second death.
> [15] If anyone's name was not found written in the Book of Life, he was thrown into the Lake of Fire.
>
> Revelation 20:11-15 NIV

If you haven't given your life to Jesus Christ, your name is not written in the Book of Life referred to above. Consequently, when your earthly body dies, your spirit will be thrown in to the Lake of Fire to be tortured for all of eternity.

I pray you do not end up there!

You don't have to, you can accept Jesus Christ into your heart and He will forgive you and write your name in the Book of Life! Won't you give Him your life?

You are but one heartbeat away from your eternity!

Chapter Three

His Message

His message is a simple one. Jesus died for us and the message is that we have all sinned and fallen short of the grace of GOD. Jesus wants you to give your life to Him, as He freely gave His life for you on the brutal cross at Calvary.

Then He commands us to love our neighbor as ourselves. Sounds simple, right?

What is GOD saying to the Churches?

The Church is a called generation, a chosen people who are to influence the world for Jesus and to shine His light into the darkness! We are to tell the Good News of His forgiveness of sin.

GOD is speaking to the Church, and to all those who are listening, as we are preparing for the battle that is soon to come!

The battle is for our souls and our eternal address, Heaven or Hell?

> [1] The revelation of Jesus Christ, which GOD gave Him to show His servants what must soon take place. He made it known by sending His Angel to His servant John,
> [2] who testifies to everything he saw, that is, the Word of GOD and the testimony of Jesus Christ.
> [3] Blessed is the one who reads the words of this prophecy, and blessed are those who hear it and take to heart what is written in it, because the time is near.

Greetings and doxology.

⁴ John,

To the seven Churches in the province of Asia:

Grace and peace to you from Him who is, and who was, and who is to come, and from the seven spirits before His throne,

> ⁵ and from Jesus Christ, who is the faithful witness, the firstborn from the dead, and the ruler of the kings of the earth. To Him who loves us and has freed us from our sins by His blood,
> ⁶ and has made us to be a kingdom and priests to serve His GOD and Father, to Him be glory and power for ever and ever! Amen.
> ⁷ Look, He is coming with the clouds, and every eye will see Him, even those who pierced Him; and all the peoples of the earth will mourn because of Him. So shall it be! Amen.
> ⁸ "I am the Alpha and the Omega," says the Lord GOD, "who is, and who was, and who is to come, the Almighty."
> ⁹ I, John, your brother and companion in the suffering and kingdom and patient endurance that are ours in Jesus, was on the island of Patmos because of the Word of GOD and the testimony of Jesus.
> ¹⁰ On the Lord's Day I was in the Spirit, and I heard behind me a loud voice like a trumpet,
> ¹¹ which said: "Write on a scroll what you see and send it to the seven Churches: to Ephesus, Smyrna, Pergamum, Thyatira, Sardis, Philadelphia and Laodicea."
> ¹² I turned around to see the voice that was speaking to me. And when I turned I saw seven golden lampstands,
> ¹³ and among the lampstands was someone "like a son of man," dressed in a robe reaching down to His feet and with a golden sash around His chest.
> ¹⁴ His head and hair were white like wool, as white as snow, and His eyes were like blazing fire.

¹⁵ His feet were like bronze glowing in a furnace, and His voice was like the sound of rushing waters.

¹⁶ In His right hand He held seven stars, and out of His mouth came a sharp double-edged sword. His face was like the sun shining in all its brilliance.

¹⁷ When I saw Him, I fell at His feet as though dead. Then He placed His right hand on me and said: "Do not be afraid. I am the First and the Last.

¹⁸ I am the Living One; I was dead, and behold I am alive for ever and ever! And I hold the keys of death and Hades."

¹⁹ "Write, therefore, what you have seen, what is now and what will take place later.

²⁰ The mystery of the seven stars that you saw in my right hand and of the seven golden lampstands is this: The seven stars are the Angels of the seven Churches, and the seven lampstands are the seven Churches."

Revelation 1 NIV

To the Church in Ephesus.

¹ "To the Angel of the Church in Ephesus write:
These are the words of Him who holds the seven stars in His right hand and walks among the seven golden lampstands:

² I know your deeds, your hard work and your perseverance. I know that you cannot tolerate wicked men, that you have tested those who claim to be apostles but are not, and have found them false.

³ You have persevered and have endured hardships for my name, and have not grown weary.

⁴ Yet I hold this against you: You have forsaken your first love.

⁵ Remember the height from which you have fallen! Repent and do the things you did at first. If you do not repent, I will come to you and remove your lampstand from its place.

⁶ But you have this in your favor: You hate the practices of the Nicolaitans, which I also hate.

⁷He who has an ear, let him hear what the Spirit says to the Churches. To Him who overcomes, I will give the right to eat from the tree of life, which is in the paradise of GOD."

To the Church in Smyrna.

⁸"To the Angel of the Church in Smyrna write:
These are the words of Him who is the First and the Last, who died and came to life again.
⁹I know your afflictions and your poverty, yet you are rich! I know the slander of those who say they are Jews and are not, but are a synagogue of Satan.
¹⁰Do not be afraid of what you are about to suffer. I tell you, the devil will put some of you in prison to test you, and you will suffer persecution for ten days. Be faithful, even to the point of death, and I will give you the crown of life.
¹¹He who has an ear, let him hear what the Spirit says to the Churches. He who overcomes will not be hurt at all by the second death."

To the Church in Pergamum.

¹²"To the Angel of the Church in Pergamum write: These are the words of Him who has the sharp, double-edged sword.
¹³I know where you live, where Satan has his throne. Yet you remain true to my name. You did not renounce your faith in me, even in the days of Antipas, my faithful witness, and who was put to death in your city, where Satan lives.
¹⁴Nevertheless, I have a few things against you: You have people there who hold to the teaching of Balaam, who taught Balak to entice the Israelites to sin by eating food sacrificed to idols and by committing sexual immorality.
¹⁵Likewise you also have those who hold to the teaching of the Nicolaitans.
¹⁶Repent therefore! Otherwise, I will soon come to you and will fight against them with the sword of my mouth.

¹⁷ He who has an ear, let him hear what the Spirit says to the Churches. To him who overcomes, I will give some of the hidden manna. I will also give him a white stone with a new name written on it, known only to him who receives it."

To the Church in Thyatira.

¹⁸ "To the Angel of the Church in Thyatira write:
These are the words of the Son of GOD, whose eyes are like blazing fire and whose feet are like burnished bronze.
¹⁹ I know your deeds, your love and faith, your service and perseverance, and that you are now doing more than you did at first.
²⁰ Nevertheless, I have this against you: You tolerate that woman Jezebel, who calls herself a prophetess. By her teaching she misleads my servants into sexual immorality and the eating of food sacrificed to idols.
²¹ I have given her time to repent of her immorality, but she is unwilling.
²² So I will cast her on a bed of suffering, and I will make those who commit adultery with her suffer intensely, unless they repent of her ways.
²³ I will strike her children dead. Then all the Churches will know that I am He who searches hearts and minds, and I will repay each of you according to your deeds.
²⁴ Now I say to the rest of you in Thyatira, to you who do not hold to her teaching and have not learned Satan's so-called deep secrets (I will not impose any other burden on you):
²⁵ Only hold on to what you have until I come.
²⁶ To him who overcomes and does my will to the end, I will give authority over the nations.
²⁷ 'He will rule them with an iron scepter; He will dash them to pieces like pottery' just as I have received authority from my Father.
²⁸ I will also give Him the morning star.
²⁹ He who has an ear, let him hear what the Spirit says to the Churches."

Revelation 2 NIV

To the Church in Sardis.

¹ "To the Angel of the Church in Sardis write:
These are the words of Him who holds the seven spirits of GOD and the seven stars. I know your deeds; you have a reputation of being alive, but you are dead.
² Wake up! Strengthen what remains and is about to die, for I have not found your deeds complete in the sight of my GOD.
³ Remember, therefore, what you have received and heard; obey it, and repent. But if you do not wake up, I will come like a thief, and you will not know at what time I will come to you.
⁴ Yet you have a few people in Sardis who have not soiled their clothes. They will walk with me, dressed in white, for they are worthy.
⁵ He who overcomes will, like them, be dressed in white. I will never blot out his name from the Book of Life, but will acknowledge his name before my Father and His Angels.
⁶ He who has an ear, let him hear what the Spirit says to the Churches."

To the Church in Philadelphia.

⁷ "To the Angel of the Church in Philadelphia write: These are the words of Him who is holy and true, who holds the key of David. What He opens no one can shut, and what He shuts no one can open.
⁸ I know your deeds. See, I have placed before you an open door that no one can shut. I know that you have little strength, yet you have kept my word and have not denied my name.
⁹ I will make those who are of the synagogue of Satan, who claim to be Jews though they are not, but are liars, I will make them come and fall down at your feet and acknowledge that I have loved you.
¹⁰ Since you have kept my command to endure patiently, I will also keep you from the hour of trial that is going to come upon the whole world to test those who live on the earth.

¹¹ I am coming soon. Hold on to what you have, so that no one will take your crown.

¹² Him who overcomes I will make a pillar in the temple of my GOD. Never again will he leave it. I will write on him the name of my GOD and the name of the city of my GOD, the New Jerusalem, which is coming down out of heaven from my GOD; and I will also write on him my new name.

¹³ He who has an ear, let him hear what the Spirit says to the Churches."

To the Church in Laodicea.

¹⁴ "To the Angel of the Church in Laodicea write: These are the words of the Amen, the faithful and true witness, the ruler of GOD's creation.

¹⁵ I know your deeds, that you are neither cold nor hot. I wish you were either one or the other!

¹⁶ So, because you are lukewarm, neither hot nor cold, I am about to spit you out of my mouth.

¹⁷ You say, 'I am rich; I have acquired wealth and do not need a thing.' But you do not realize that you are wretched, pitiful, poor, blind and naked.

¹⁸ I counsel you to buy from me gold refined in the fire, so you can become rich; and white clothes to wear, so you can cover your shameful nakedness; and salve to put on your eyes, so you can see.

¹⁹ Those whom I love I rebuke and discipline. So be earnest, and repent.

²⁰ Here I am! I stand at the door and knock. If anyone hears my voice and opens the door, I will come in and eat with him, and he with me.

²¹ To him who overcomes, I will give the right to sit with me on my throne, just as I overcame and sat down with my Father on His throne.

²² He who has an ear, let him hear what the Spirit says to the Churches."

Revelation 3 NIV

GOD is calling His Churches to wake up!

We are supposed to be a light to the world and a giver of all good things!

GOD's message is the same as in the beginning of time.

He calls each of us to His heart, to hear His message to love one another, to tell of the Good News of Jesus Christ; His life, His suffering, His atonement and His sacrifice for our Sins.

Jesus is the way to make right what the Serpent in the Garden of Eden did, to cause the world to go in the wrong direction and out of GOD's plan for us.

Satan seeks to destroy the multitudes and his tactics are lying, deception and temptations, all which caused Adam and Eve to fall, and is presently causing the world to still fall under his wicked curses.

When I look at our world today, I see such thoughtlessness in the lives of people everywhere!

Our streets and neighborhoods are littered with the disposables of society. Many people cast off things they no longer regard as needed or wanted in their lives. It is harder to find true honesty and character in people today, who live solely for their own purposes.

I tend to believe that they are not bad people, but instead they are a hurting people, a generation who is sickened by their lives and the uncertainty of tomorrow.

Many live without any hope for their future and they don't examine where their life is headed.

For every bad, there is good and there are many people on the earth today who are kind-hearted, sincere, truthful, and filled with the love of GOD.

You may also know people with the same characteristics, but have not yet placed their trust in Jesus Christ and do not refer to themselves as "Christians" but rather as just "good people."

I believe this is the majority of our population today and I must tell you that although you may be a very "good" person, that will not buy you an eternity into Heaven!

Only those who put their faith and trust in Jesus Christ will ever enter Heaven's gates!

I know many people disagree with this truth. I must keep reminding myself that not all will come to the saving grace of Jesus Christ, even though that is my heart's cry!

I remember praying for GOD to give me the burden for soul-winning and GOD certainly did answer that prayer!

So, in everything you ask GOD for, be mindful that He does give you the desires of your heart. You may not get an answer to prayer the way you think you want it, but sometimes unanswered prayers are really the best answers of all.

So is there "Truth" in Reality?

I believe that is what so many are seeking in this hour, and to find the truth, in the midst of the reality we live in, is not always an easy task!

Generations have gone forth since the creation of the world and the plan that GOD had for our lives seems so far away and distant in our minds. It is easier to "go with the flow" so to speak and to ignore the profanity of so many, or the nuances of a society that is led to hold a belief system that seeks to please only themselves.

There are even Churches forming everywhere that say, we accept you, your lifestyle, your views, for there is no "right" or "wrong" anymore.

These Churches proclaim to be a "spiritual awakening" kind of Church who will endorse whatever you believe about life and the hereafter. They claim everyone is a Spirit being, which is the truth, but then they twist the idea by claiming that we will all dwell together in unity at the end of time.

They claim there is no Hell, but living on earth is Hell. What a lie!!

It is a comfort to those who do not want to conform to anyone's laws or views, and want to live their life as they please. It is a real ego stroke from the devil himself, so that he can lead you straight to Hell's gates and forever torment you.

Unity in the Body of Christ.

> [1] As a prisoner for the Lord, then, I urge you to live a life worthy of the calling you have received.

² Be completely humble and gentle; be patient, bearing with one another in love.

³ Make every effort to keep the unity of the Spirit through the bond of peace.

⁴ There is one body and one Spirit, just as you were called to one hope when you were called

⁵ one Lord, one faith, one baptism;

⁶ one GOD and Father of all; who is over all and through all and in all.

⁷ But to each one of us grace has been given as Christ apportioned it.

⁸ This is why it says: "When He ascended on high, He led captives in His train and gave gifts to men."

⁹ (What does "He ascended" mean except that He also descended to the lower, earthly regions?

¹⁰ He who descended is the very one who ascended higher than all the heavens, in order to fill the whole universe.)

¹¹ It was He, who gave some to be apostles, some to be prophets, some to be evangelists, and some to be pastors and teachers,

¹² to prepare GOD's people for works of service, so that the body of Christ may be built up,

¹³ until we all reach unity in the faith and in the knowledge of the Son of GOD and become mature, attaining to the whole measure of the fullness of Christ.

¹⁴ Then we will no longer be infants, tossed back and forth by the waves, and blown here and there by every wind of teaching and by the cunning and craftiness of men in their deceitful scheming.

¹⁵ Instead, speaking the truth in love, we will in all things grow up into Him who is the Head, that is, Christ.

¹⁶ From Him the whole body, joined and held together by every supporting ligament, grows and builds itself up in love, as each part does its work.

Ephesians 4:1-16 NIV

Each Church, each denomination has a purpose and a calling that is their own. We are each a part of the Body of Christ, each having our own calling and work to be done to save people from their sins. It is sad to me when one denomination points fingers and exalts themselves over another one.

We must be mindful that GOD is in control and if a Church is teaching a false doctrine, GOD's wrath will visit them. We are; however, to adhere to the Words of the Holy Bible and to heed the instructions therein.

No matter the denomination you belong to as a Believer, read your Bible and examine the Scriptures for yourselves.

Never let a preacher, priest, evangelist, prophet, apostle, teacher or others teach you something that is not in the Bible itself. If it is not found in Scripture, you could be dealing with a "sheep in wolves clothing" and when you reach Heaven; your eternal destination is not dependent on your Church membership, or your denominational beliefs. It all comes down to you and the decision you make in your own heart. Your parents can't save you, your Christian neighbor can't save you, and I can't save you, only you can do that by trusting in Jesus Christ.

Have you trusted your heart to Jesus Christ and confessed and repented of your sins? If not, then you are not a Christian. A Christian is someone who has trusted in Jesus Christ and no one else.

A Christian is not perfect, and they follow to the best of their ability, the teachings of Jesus Christ. They are usually considered "good people," but that doesn't grant them an eternity in Heaven, only repenting and accepting Jesus Christ grants them an eternity in Heaven.

Generations before us taught their children and the neighbor's children that there were consequences for their actions. We held to a belief system that the majority of Americans adhered to. America was even founded by Christian leaders, with Christian principles and much was written into law from the Bible itself.

We now live in a society that wants to eliminate the Ten Commandments, the Bible, praying in public, and most importantly, GOD Himself.

But I really wonder if that is the heart of most people, or just a few?

GOD is sending us wake-up calls, and if we don't heed His many warnings, I am afraid He will take His mighty hand of protection away from us and His wrath will one day be poured out in His full measure of fury.

GOD cares about mankind and our futures, and we should to!

There are absolute "rights" and "wrongs" and it saddens me that so many live on the fringe of life, not wanting to abide by any Godly expectations. They want to live as a law unto themselves.

Many want to live as they please, and to heck with the rest of the world. This type of thinking and living is so dangerous because it leaves no room for righteous and holy living, and it opens the door for the devil to come in and deceive so many.

I know many in this world say, "Who cares?" We all have a right to be who we are in this world!

This is true, GOD made each of us unique; there are no two individuals alike. We are each destined for an exact purpose and no-one is equipped as anyone else, we each have a calling and a purpose for our life.

I believe the majority of people are seeking a better life, a better future for themselves and their family. You probably already know many who are seeking GOD and have a tender heart.

I see a lot of people who are broken and hurt by their lives and they seem distant, prideful and hard-hearted. However, if you peel back the layers of their walk of life, you will find a hurting soul who longs to be loved! They have been hardened by the brutalities of life and the injustices they have incurred.

It is not easy to stay soft in this hardened world we live in.

My desire is to encourage everyone to have a deeper and closer walk with GOD, so He will speak to your heart and tell you that He loves you!

Your past doesn't matter; each day is spent and is to be forgotten! You can change and no matter the lifestyle you find yourself living right now, know that you are worthy of His love for you! You don't deserve it, no one does, but He loves you with an everlasting love, if you will only reach out for Him, He will meet you right where you are!

We can all be a "light" for the world, full of love and compassion, which is what GOD created all of us to be, if only we will walk in His love and His examples! We cannot do that if we first don't accept His love, His forgiveness and repent of our sins.

Those who are living and hiding themselves in drugs, alcohol, pornography, sorcery, and witchcraft can be free to really live. They don't have to have those strongholds over them in their life; GOD does have a purpose for each one of us! They may feel satisfied with their lives and not even realize that they have bondages on them, especially if they have never known any other lifestyle, and no one has told them about a GOD who loves them deeply and longs to talk with them.

What is your reality? Do you want to change your life and come to GOD?

GOD wants us to pull off our masks and get real. Get real with Him and get real with yourself. Are you truly happy and fulfilled with the choices you have made in your own life?

It has been taught that Jesus came to abolish the old laws and to give us a freedom that we don't have to live under the curse of the law.

Faith or Observance of the Law.

> 1 You foolish Galatians! Who has bewitched you? Before your very eyes Jesus Christ was clearly portrayed as crucified.
> 2 I would like to learn just one thing from you: Did you receive the Spirit by observing the law, or by believing what you heard?
> 3 Are you so foolish? After beginning with the Spirit, are you now trying to attain your goal by human effort?
> 4 Have you suffered so much for nothing, if it really was for nothing?
> 5 Does GOD give you His Spirit and work miracles among you because you observe the law, or because you believe what you heard?
> 6 Consider Abraham: "He believed GOD, and it was credited to him as righteousness."
> 7 Understand, then, that those who believe are children of Abraham.

⁸ The Scripture foresaw that GOD would justify the Gentiles by faith, and announced the gospel in advance to Abraham: "All nations will be blessed through you."

⁹ So those who have faith are blessed along with Abraham, the man of faith.

¹⁰ All who rely on observing the law are under a curse, for it is written: "Cursed is everyone who does not continue to do everything written in the Book of the Law."

¹¹ Clearly no one is justified before GOD by the law, because, "The righteous will live by faith."

¹² The law is not based on faith; on the contrary, "The man who does these things will live by them."

¹³ Christ redeemed us from the curse of the law by becoming a curse for us, for it is written: "Cursed is everyone who is hung on a tree."

¹⁴ He redeemed us in order that the blessing given to Abraham might come to the Gentiles through Christ Jesus, so that by faith we might receive the promise of the Spirit.

¹⁵ Brothers, let me take an example from everyday life. Just as no one can set aside or add to a human covenant that has been duly established, so it is in this case.

¹⁶ The promises were spoken to Abraham and to his seed. The Scripture does not say "and to seeds," meaning many people, but "and to your seed," meaning one person, who is Christ.

¹⁷ What I mean is this: The law, introduced 430 years later, does not set aside the covenant previously established by GOD and thus do away with the promise.

¹⁸ For if the inheritance depends on the law, then it no longer depends on a promise; but GOD in His grace gave it to Abraham through a promise.

¹⁹ What, then, was the purpose of the law? It was added because of transgressions until the Seed to whom the promise referred had come. The law was put into effect through Angels by a mediator.

²⁰ A mediator, however, does not represent just one party; but GOD is one.

²¹ Is the law, therefore, opposed to the promises of GOD? Absolutely not! For if a law had been given that could impart life, then righteousness would certainly have come by the law.

²² But the Scripture declares that the whole world is a prisoner of sin, so that what was promised, being given through faith in Jesus Christ, might be given to those who believe.

²³ Before this faith came, we were held prisoners by the law, locked up until faith should be revealed.

²⁴ So the law was put in charge to lead us to Christ that we might be justified by faith.

²⁵ Now that faith has come, we are no longer under the supervision of the law.

²⁶ You are all sons of GOD through faith in Christ Jesus,

²⁷ for all of you who were baptized into Christ have clothed yourselves with Christ.

²⁸ There is neither Jew nor Greek, slave nor free, male nor female, for you are all one in Christ Jesus.

²⁹ If you belong to Christ, then you are Abraham's seed, and heirs according to the promise.

Galatians 3 NIV

Jesus did not die to give us a license to steal, kill and destroy each other or ourselves. Jesus came to fulfill the law and to fulfill prophesies given by the prophets of the Old Testament. He sacrificed Himself for us!

¹⁵ For this reason Christ is the mediator of a new covenant, that those who are called may receive the promised eternal inheritance, now that He has died as a ransom to set them free from the sins committed under the first covenant.

¹⁶ In the case of a Will, it is necessary to prove the death of the one, who made it,

¹⁷ because a Will is in force only when somebody has died; it never takes effect while the one who made it is living.

¹⁸ This is why even the first covenant was not put into effect without blood.

¹⁹ When Moses had proclaimed every commandment of the law to all the people, he took the blood of calves, together with water, scarlet wool and branches of hyssop, and sprinkled the scroll and all the people.

²⁰ He said, "This is the blood of the covenant, which GOD has commanded you to keep."

²¹ In the same way, he sprinkled with the blood both the tabernacle and everything used in its ceremonies.

²² In fact, the law requires that nearly everything be cleansed with blood and without the shedding of blood there is no forgiveness.

²³ It was necessary, then, for the copies of the heavenly things to be purified with these sacrifices, but the heavenly things themselves with better sacrifices than these.

²⁴ For Christ did not enter a man-made sanctuary that was only a copy of the true one; He entered heaven itself, now to appear for us in GOD's presence.

²⁵ Nor did He enter heaven to offer himself again and again, the way the high priest enters the Most Holy Place every year with blood that is not His own.

²⁶ Then Christ would have had to suffer many times since the creation of the world. But now He has appeared once for all at the end of the ages to do away with sin by the sacrifice of Himself.

²⁷ Just as man is destined to die once, and after that to face judgment,

²⁸ so Christ was sacrificed once to take away the sins of many people; and He will appear a second time, not to bear sin, but to bring salvation to those who are waiting for him.

Hebrews 9 NIV

GOD had to send His precious Son, Jesus Christ to the cross because we can't make atonement for our sins and be purified, except by the blood. When GOD abolished the laws of sacrifice, He had to bring forth a more holy, lasting sacrifice, once for all, until the end of time.

This sacrifice was and is Jesus Christ, who now lives to intercede to the Father GOD on our behalf. He is seated at the right hand of the Father.

Jesus Christ hears your prayers and He has sent the Holy Spirit to be a comfort and a wise counselor to us, for our every decision. We cannot ever earn Heaven, or access to our Father GOD, without going through Jesus Christ.

Jesus Christ is the door to salvation, won't you seek Him?

> 22 Then Jesus went through the towns and villages, teaching as He made His way to Jerusalem.
> 23 Someone asked him, "Lord, are only a few people going to be saved?" He said to them,
> 24 "Make every effort to enter through the narrow door, because many, I tell you, will try to enter and will not be able to.
> 25 Once the owner of the house gets up and closes the door, you will stand outside knocking and pleading, 'Sir, open the door for us.' But He will answer, 'I don't know you or where you come from.'
> 26 Then you will say, 'We ate and drank with you, and you taught in our streets.'
> 27 But He will reply, 'I don't know you or where you come from. Away from me, all you evildoers!'
> 28 There will be weeping there, and gnashing of teeth, when you see Abraham, Isaac and Jacob and all the prophets in the kingdom of GOD, but you yourselves thrown out.
> 29 People will come from east and west and north and south, and will take their places at the feast in the kingdom of GOD.
> 30 Indeed there are those who are last who will be first, and first who will be last."
>
> Luke 13:22-30 NIV

You see, many will read these words and be quick to repent. They will realize that they are indeed a sinner and will accept Jesus Christ as their Savior.

If we all were to examine our hearts and line up our character by the Ten Commandments, we would discover that all of us have sinned. There is not one person that is exempt.

The Ten Commandments.

[1] And GOD spoke all these words:
[2] "I am the LORD your GOD, who brought you out of Egypt, out of the land of slavery."
[3] "You shall have no other Gods before me."
[4] "You shall not make for yourself an idol in the form of anything in heaven above or on the earth beneath or in the waters below."
[5] "You shall not bow down to them or worship them; for I, the LORD your GOD, am a jealous GOD, punishing the children for the sin of the fathers to the third and fourth generation of those who hate me,
[6] but showing love to a thousand generations of those who love me and keep my commandments."
[7] "You shall not misuse the name of the LORD your GOD, for the LORD will not hold anyone guiltless who misuses His name."
[8] "Remember the Sabbath day by keeping it holy.
[9] Six days you shall labor and do all your work,
[10] but the seventh day is a Sabbath to the LORD your GOD. On it you shall not do any work, neither you, nor your son or daughter, nor your manservant or maidservant, nor your animals, nor the alien within your gates.
[11] For in six days the LORD made the heavens and the earth, the sea, and all that is in them, but he rested on the seventh day. Therefore the LORD blessed the Sabbath day and made it holy."
[12] "Honor your father and your mother, so that you may live long in the land the LORD your GOD is giving you."
[13] "You shall not murder."
[14] "You shall not commit adultery."
[15] "You shall not steal."
[16] "You shall not give false testimony against your neighbor."

17 "You shall not covet your neighbor's house. You shall not covet your neighbor's wife, or his manservant or maidservant, his ox or donkey, or anything that belongs to your neighbor."

18 When the people saw the thunder and lightning and heard the trumpet and saw the mountain in smoke, they trembled with fear. They stayed at a distance

19 and said to Moses, "Speak to us yourself and we will listen. But do not have GOD speak to us or we will die."

20 Moses said to the people, "Do not be afraid. GOD has come to test you, so that the fear of GOD will be with you to keep you from sinning."

21 The people remained at a distance, while Moses approached the thick darkness where GOD was.

22 Then the LORD said to Moses, "Tell the Israelites this: 'You have seen for yourselves that I have spoken to you from heaven:'

23 Do not make any Gods to be alongside me; do not make for yourselves Gods of silver or Gods of gold."

Exodus 20:1-23 NIV

When we examine the Ten Commandments there are a few that each of us have committed sometime in our lives. Such as lying, stealing and committing adultery.

Jesus tells us that if we look upon someone with lust in our eyes, we have already committed adultery in our heart, and it is the same as if we actually committed the sexual act. What about the little "white" lies we often tell our friends or co-workers?

27 "You have heard that it was said, 'Do not commit adultery.'

28 But I tell you that anyone who looks at a woman lustfully has already committed adultery with her in his heart.

29 If your right eye causes you to sin, gouge it out and throw it away. It is better for you to lose one part of your body than for your whole body to be thrown into hell.

30 And if your right hand causes you to sin, cut it off and throw it away. It is better for you to lose one part of your body than for your whole body to go into hell."

Matthew 5:27-30 NIV

As you can see from the above Scriptures, GOD is serious about sin and its effect on our walk with Him. He wants us to fellowship with Him daily and to seek His Will for our lives. He also reminds us that no sin is greater than any other, except for blasphemy of the Holy Spirit, which is a serious offense to GOD.

I point all this out to you so that you can be convicted of your sins and demonstrate to you that you have not lived a perfect and sinless life.

No one has and that is the reason Jesus came to the earth, to redeem us from the chains of Hell.

> 43 "You have heard that it was said, 'Love your neighbor and hate your enemy.'"
> 44 But I tell you: "Love your enemies and pray for those who persecute you;
> 45 That you may be sons of your Father in heaven. He causes His sun to rise on the evil and the good, and sends rain on the righteous and the unrighteous.
> 46 If you love those who love you, what reward will you get? Are not even the tax collectors doing that?
> 47 And if you greet only your brothers, what are you doing more than others? Do not even pagans do that?
> 48 Be perfect, therefore, as your heavenly Father is perfect."
>
> Matthew 5:43-48 NIV

Perhaps many will think I'm a fool or just plain crazy to write to you this way and certainly there will be many others who will believe that I am deceived and wrong in my thinking and they will walk away without their heart's being changed.

They will not accept the free gift of salvation from Jesus Christ; they will continue to live their lives as they did before.

It may seem like not much of a risk, if you don't believe in a life hereafter or Hell. Perhaps you know in your heart there is a Hell, but you cannot convince yourself to believe.

I pray you love yourself enough to listen to your own heartbeat and know that when it beats for the last time, you have no time left to make this important decision to surrender your life to Jesus Christ.

²¹ But now a righteousness from GOD, apart from the law, has been made known, to which the Law and the Prophets testify.
²² This righteousness from GOD comes through faith in Jesus Christ to all who believe. There is no difference,
²³ for all have sinned and fall short of the glory of GOD,
²⁴ and are justified freely by His grace through the redemption that came by Christ Jesus.
²⁵ GOD presented Him as a sacrifice of atonement, through faith in His blood. He did this to demonstrate His justice, because in His forbearance He had left the sins committed beforehand unpunished.
²⁶ He did it to demonstrate His justice at the present time, so as to be just and the one who justifies those who have faith in Jesus.
Romans 3:21-26 NIV

Many have gone before me to share this message, and many will go after me!

The important thing is to recognize the truth, to seek Jesus Christ and to open your heart and mind to the "what if's."

What if this author is right?

What has my life been up to now? Am I really, truly a sinner?

Please know that *all* have sinned, you are not a horrible person and certainly not the only one in this world that needs to repent!

Everyone needs Jesus Christ, but many will be too proud to seek Him and they will not turn their lives over to Him.

There will be many who will reject the truth in this book and they will spend eternity in Hell.

This is the saddest tragedy in life that I know of!

I wish I could write the right words to make every person who is reading this book believe on Jesus Christ and miss the judgments of GOD.

To give your life to Jesus Christ, all you have to do is repeat this prayer with a sincere heart.

"Lord Jesus, I know that I am a Sinner and that I need you in my life. Jesus, come into my heart and forgive me of all my sins. Help me to live for you. I acknowledge that you are truly the Son of GOD and the only way through which I can be saved. Lord, I believe, save me Lord Jesus. Amen."

I pray GOD will continue to give me the words and strength to convince you to turn your life over to Jesus Christ, if you aren't convinced yet that GOD loves you with an everlasting love.

For the director of music. Of David. A psalm.

> [1] O LORD, you have searched me and you know me.
> [2] You know when I sit and when I rise; you perceive my thoughts from afar.
> [3] You discern my going out and my lying down; you are familiar with all my ways.
> [4] Before a word is on my tongue you know it completely, O LORD.
> [5] You hem me in, behind and before; you have laid your hand upon me.
> [6] Such knowledge is too wonderful for me, too lofty for me to attain.
> [7] Where can I go from your Spirit? Where can I flee from your presence?
> [8] If I go up to the heavens, you are there; if I make my bed in the depths, you are there.
> [9] If I rise on the wings of the dawn, if I settle on the far side of the sea,
> [10] even there your hand will guide me, your right hand will hold me fast.
> [11] If I say, "Surely the darkness will hide me and the light become night around me,"
> [12] even the darkness will not be dark to you; the night will shine like the day, for darkness is as light to you.
> [13] For you created my inmost being; you knit me together in my mother's womb.
> [14] I praise you because I am fearfully and wonderfully made; your works are wonderful, I know that full well.

¹⁵ My frame was not hidden from you when I was made in the secret place. When I was woven together in the depths of the earth,
¹⁶ your eyes saw my unformed body. All the days ordained for me were written in your book before one of them came to be.
¹⁷ How precious to me are your thoughts, O GOD! How vast is the sum of them!
¹⁸ Were I to count them; they would outnumber the grains of sand. When I awake, I am still with you.
¹⁹ If only you would slay the wicked, O GOD! Away from me, you bloodthirsty men!
²⁰ They speak of you with evil intent; your adversaries misuse your name.
²¹ Do I not hate those who hate you, O LORD, and abhor those who rise up against you?
²² I have nothing but hatred for them; I count them my enemies.
²³ Search me, O GOD, and know my heart; test me and know my anxious thoughts.
²⁴ See if there is any offensive way in me, and lead me in the way everlasting.

Psalm 139 NIV

Just as King David penned these words so long ago, you can have your own writings, welling up deep within you, as you give your life over to Jesus Christ.

He will never leave you or forsake you, ever!

If you already belong to the Lord Jesus, then you understand the depth of what I am speaking about and how much He gives us comfort in the midst of our storms! He will carry us through to the other side, to the joy that is unspeakable and a peace that will never leave us.

Are you longing for His peace?

Chapter Four

A Call for Holy Living

*G*OD is calling each of us to live a Holy life before Him.

The commandments of our Lord are not unbearable, but are a sacrifice of our love demonstrated to Him when we live within His requirements.

This was written to me in this day and hour that we now live in.

March 5, 2005
3:10 a.m.

Many false prophets have come in my name and are now preaching in the pulpits. They deceive my Church.

Go forth with the message that I am watching and will deal with them treacherously for they are misleading the multitudes down the wrong path. They excuse their deeds for my grace, I will not contend with them forever.

People need to live holy lives, not on the fence of indecision. They must stand for something; they are lukewarm, seeking a position of authority. They seek the approval of men, they are an abomination in my sight, I will remove them in my time.

I have warned my people in my Holy Word. Tell them to watch and pray; the time is short. The trumpet is ready to sound, the Angels are rejoicing, the harvest is near, it is almost at the door.

My people perish for lack of knowledge, they only need to seek me and spend time in the quiet secret place and I will shower them with my love.

They must turn from their wicked ways before the bridegroom comes for His bride, or the door will forever be shut on them and I will hear their screams, their cries will ascend into Heaven, but I will not be moved.

I have sent my Prophets to warn them, they are stiff-necked, an obstinate people who want to go their own way, because of this they will receive unto themselves eternal judgment.

My anointed ones who love me will dwell with me for all eternity in the place I have prepared for them. I see their obedience and their heart; they live their life in surrender of my good pleasure.

I am well pleased with them.

They pray without ceasing and they consult with me about their life and their desires.

I love the intimate fellowship of a surrendered life.

There are so few. My heart breaks to see so many carelessly walking onto the path of destruction; they are a God unto themselves.

Shalom, my beloved. You are mine.

Can't you see the heart of GOD in the above message and how it is breaking over the lost souls walking on this earth?

GOD wants us to come to Him, to talk and walk with Him and all He asks in return is for us to live a life pleasing and Holy unto Him. He isn't trying to attach a "ball and chain" to your leg, He knows what is best for each of us and if we would lay down our agenda's, He will give us a peace that is full of joy unending. I truly believe that is why I've been called to write this book, to save so many from the course their life is taking towards Hell.

Won't you help me spread this message?

> [1] In the presence of GOD and of Christ Jesus, who will judge the living and the dead, and in view of His appearing and His kingdom, I give you this charge:
> [2] Preach the Word; be prepared in season and out of season; correct, rebuke and encourage, with great patience and careful instruction.

³ For the time will come when men will not put up with sound doctrine. Instead, to suit their own desires, they will gather around them a great number of teachers to say what their itching ears want to hear.

⁴ They will turn their ears away from the truth and turn aside to myths.

⁵ But you, keep your head in all situations, endure hardship, do the work of an evangelist, and discharge all the duties of your ministry.

2 Timothy 4: 1-5 NIV

The above was given to the Apostle Paul in the New Testament, which confirms the message that GOD gave me in the preceding message.

Now, let's review the below which was written to the Servant Moses, in the Old Testament time before the birth of Jesus Christ.

¹ The LORD said to Moses,

² "Speak to the entire assembly of Israel and say to them: 'Be holy because I, the LORD your GOD, am holy.'"

³ "Each of you must respect his mother and father, and you must observe my Sabbaths. I am the LORD your GOD."

⁴ "Do not turn to idols or make Gods of cast metal for yourselves. I am the LORD your GOD."

⁵ "When you sacrifice a fellowship offering to the LORD, sacrifice it in such a way that it will be accepted on your behalf.

⁶ It shall be eaten on the day you sacrifice it or on the next day; anything left over until the third day must be burned up.

⁷ If any of it is eaten on the third day, it is impure and will not be accepted.

⁸ Whoever eats it will be held responsible because he has desecrated what is holy to the LORD; that person must be cut off from his people.

⁹ When you reap the harvest of your land, do not reap to the very edges of your field or gather the gleanings of your harvest.

10 Do not go over your vineyard a second time or pick up the grapes that have fallen. Leave them for the poor and the alien. I am the LORD your GOD."

11 "Do not steal. Do not lie. Do not deceive one another."

12 "Do not swear falsely by my name and so profane the name of your GOD. I am the LORD."

13 "Do not defraud your neighbor or rob him. Do not hold back the wages of a hired man overnight."

14 "Do not curse the deaf or put a stumbling block in front of the blind, but fear your GOD. I am the LORD."

15 "Do not pervert justice; do not show partiality to the poor or favoritism to the great, but judge your neighbor fairly."

16 "Do not go about spreading slander among your people. Do not do anything that endangers your neighbor's life. I am the LORD."

17 "Do not hate your brother in your heart. Rebuke your neighbor frankly so you will not share in his guilt."

18 "Do not seek revenge or bear a grudge against one of your people, but love your neighbor as yourself. I am the LORD."

19 "Keep my decrees. Do not mate different kinds of animals. Do not plant your field with two kinds of seed. Do not wear clothing woven of two kinds of material."

20 "If a man sleeps with a woman who is a slave girl promised to another man but who has not been ransomed or given her freedom, there must be due punishment. Yet they are not to be put to death, because she had not been freed.

21 The man, however, must bring a ram to the entrance to the Tent of Meeting for a guilt offering to the LORD.

22 With the ram of the guilt offering the priest is to make atonement for him before the LORD for the sin he has committed, and his sin will be forgiven."

23 "When you enter the land and plant any kind of fruit tree, regard its fruit as forbidden. For three years you are to consider it forbidden; it must not be eaten.

24 In the fourth year all its fruit will be holy, an offering of praise to the LORD.

[25] But in the fifth year you may eat its fruit. In this way your harvest will be increased. I am the LORD your GOD."

[26] "Do not eat any meat with the blood still in it. Do not practice divination or sorcery."

[27] "Do not cut the hair at the sides of your head or clip off the edges of your beard."

[28] "Do not cut your bodies for the dead or put tattoo marks on yourselves. I am the LORD."

[29] "Do not degrade your daughter by making her a prostitute, or the land will turn to prostitution and be filled with wickedness."

[30] "Observe my Sabbaths and have reverence for my sanctuary. I am the LORD."

[31] "Do not turn to mediums or seek out spiritists, for you will be defiled by them. I am the LORD your GOD."

[32] "Rise in the presence of the aged, show respect for the elderly and revere your GOD. I am the LORD."

[33] "When an alien lives with you in your land, do not mistreat him.

[34] The alien living with you must be treated as one of your native-born. Love him as yourself, for you were aliens in Egypt. I am the LORD your GOD."

[35] "Do not use dishonest standards when measuring length, weight or quantity.

[36] Use honest scales and honest weights, an honest ephah and an honest hin. I am the LORD your GOD, who brought you out of Egypt."

[37] "Keep all my decrees and all my laws and follow them. I am the LORD."

Leviticus 19 NIV

We live in an age and time that is classified as the "New Testament" period, the time in which Jesus came and walked the earth and abolished the laws of old.

Some people say the "Old Testament" is not relevant in our lives today. However, I disagree and have learned much from studying the Old Testament.

I have also learned much from meditating with GOD and listening to His voice.

It is true that the previous Scriptures refer to a time before the crucifixion of Jesus Christ and He abolished the old laws of sacrifice. However, I do believe that the rest of the commandments from the preceding Scriptures from GOD should still be lived in solemn reverence today, and we should strive to live Holy lives for our Lord GOD.

The Law could not make us righteous and that is why GOD sent His Son, Jesus to the cross, because the laws could not make us in right standing and a better covenant had to be made for us.

Saying that, it is a debated question of whether we are still to abide by the Law of Moses or the Grace of GOD. I believe the Laws of sacrifice are abolished completely and I think we should thank GOD for the sacrificial giving of His Son, Jesus on the cross.

The Bible also tells us that Jesus did not come to abolish the law, but to fulfill the law.

I also believe we should strive to abide by the Ten Commandments, for they are not burdensome, but were given to us by GOD so it would go well with us.

The Ten Commandments cannot make us perfect or save us; only by the grace of Jesus Christ can we be saved!

I think of the Ten Commandments as a measuring stick to help us see when we miss the mark, so we can repent and ask for forgiveness for our sins!

In studying the Old Testament you will learn of people's lives and the walks they took on their journeys. It is a fascinating lesson of their lives and the trials they endured, much like the trials we endure today. People really are not much different today, as they were in the generations before us.

Therefore, I believe that we can glean much from listening to the voice of GOD and spending time in His Word of the Old Testament. You will read of wars, famines, pestilences and victories. You will read of rapes, murders, defeats, genealogies, traditions of men and the values they placed on their families and lives.

The Old Testament and the New Testament are given as an entire Bible and GOD commands us not to remove or add anything to these books, as you will read in the following Scriptures.

> [18] I warn everyone who hears the words of the prophecy of this book: If anyone adds anything to them, God will add to him the plagues described in this book.
> [19] And if anyone takes words away from this book of prophecy, God will take away from him his share in the tree of life and in the holy city, which are described in this book.
> [20] He who testifies to these things says, "Yes, I am coming soon." Amen. Come, Lord Jesus.
> [21] The grace of the Lord Jesus be with God's people. Amen.
>
> Revelation 22:18-21 NIV

Therefore, I am careful not to add anything to the Scriptures I included in this book, and also to not take away and use (.......) to leave out words in the Scriptures. I live in awe and reverential fear of my GOD and I pray you will also.

I realize that everything belongs to the Lord, just as the words of this book are inspired by GOD, and I am a living vessel for Him to communicate through. I do not take this responsibility lightly, but am humbled that He loves me and He trusts me with His words.

Recently, He has been writing through me to warn of the coming days ahead and His wrath that will be poured out on the earth.

This is the same message He wrote through the apostles and prophets of old; the same message throughout the Bible, so I can accurately and sincerely claim these messages are indeed from the heart of GOD.

GOD continues to remind me that our days are short before His appearing and that there are many things I am yet to do for the furtherance of His Kingdom.

He also reminds me of the condition of a society that is deep in sin and living a life outside of what He had planned for us. GOD's plan was for us to live a holy life, upright and peaceful between a man and a woman.

March 17, 2005
5:10 a.m.

My beloved,

Those who seek me will find me when they seek me with all their heart. I am not far away, but very close. I long to touch my people, but my power is too great. Many fall under my power as I draw closer to them.

Do not be afraid of this power, it will work much miracles in your life. However, do not be confused, Satan can also display great and mighty things, he has the power to deceive many.

But you are a called and chosen vessel; I will not let him deceive you. But those who turn away from my commands and my love, I will give them over to the devil. I have no pleasure in fellowshipping with the fools of this world.

They are bitter, they complain and they do not receive from me because they cannot even see the many times I have spared their life!

They are an abomination to me.

I am a jealous GOD, a consuming fire. My love is greater than anything they have ever known, yet they reject me, they think they know what is best for their life.

Why they do not even know what tomorrow will bring.

I have their days numbered. I know the beginning from the end, but I will not force anyone to follow me. That would not be love! Instead, I wait with patience; I do not want to see any perish in the Lake of Fire. Multitudes will find their destiny there; that was not my plan for them.

Many harm themselves each day, I see the neglect they put on their bodies, the harsh treatment, and this should not be so.

Their body was not designed to be despised or glorified. It is a means by which to travel amongst each other. Do not look at the body to be led astray, many beautiful bodies are filled with deception and are snares from the devil.

My Son was not put in a beautiful body; it would have hindered His message. He was not becoming, but lowly and humble. These I desire, they don't get caught up in self, they do my work well.

Where there is vanity, there is pride and pride goeth before a fall. Satan deceives many by making them believe if only they were more attractive. Man looks at the appearance, but I look at the heart. Nothing is hidden from me.

I require you represent me well, in proper dress and let your beauty shine through. Tattoos and piercings I do not like, they subject the body to disgrace.

Each person is different, there are no two alike. I formed each person to be my special child. They abuse their bodies with markings; they take away the specialness I designed them for. It is a mark of the beast, it is Satan's way of showing me that my people disregard their bodies and so disregard me.

Warn the people that I am not pleased with the much mutilation of their flesh. I will forgive them if they draw near to me and repent, but the body I did not design for such unholiness.

The world is becoming a most wretched place. People do not receive their destinies, they don't even seek me.

Vengeance is mine, I will repay saith the LORD.

I have much to say about this. For now, close the book and rest. I see your heart my beloved, rest in me. I am well pleased with you.

Shalom.

As you can see from this message above, GOD's heart is breaking over a society that disregards Him and the price His precious Son, Yeshua paid for their freedom from the bondages of their sin.

I also want to clear up any misconceptions that GOD referred to as a tattoo being a "mark of the beast" as He refers to above. This is a parable of GOD and the actual "mark of the beast" will be applied in the days written about in Revelation, Chapter 13, as you will see below. This is the timeframe of the tribulation period. Anyone not following Jesus Christ and pledges an allegiance to the "anti-christ" will receive a mark, either on their right hand or their forehead.

> [11] Then I saw another beast, coming out of the earth. He had two horns like a lamb, but he spoke like a dragon.

¹² He exercised all the authority of the first beast on his behalf, and made the earth and its inhabitants worship the first beast, whose fatal wound had been healed.

¹³ And he performed great and miraculous signs, even causing fire to come down from heaven to earth in full view of men.

¹⁴ Because of the signs he was given power to do on behalf of the first beast, he deceived the inhabitants of the earth. He ordered them to set up an image in honor of the beast who was wounded by the sword and yet lived.

¹⁵ He was given power to give breath to the image of the first beast, so that it could speak and cause all who refused to worship the image to be killed.

¹⁶ He also forced everyone, small and great, rich and poor, free and slave, to receive a mark on his right hand or on his forehead;

¹⁷ So that no one could buy or sell unless he had the mark, which is the name of the beast or the number of his name.

¹⁸ This calls for wisdom. If anyone has insight, let him calculate the number of the beast, for it is man's number. His number is 666.

Revelation 13:11-18 NIV

If we are alive during this period, I caution anyone who witnesses someone exalting themselves, and coming as a Leader known throughout the world, to be reminded of what you have just read in Revelation. It is very precise in pointing knowledge for us to recognize.

This "beast" will be someone who comes forth in the name of "peace and goodwill" and will suffer a head wound which will mysteriously be healed. Watch and be careful that you are not deceived by such a person and take his "mark," no matter how innocent or wonderful they may seem to you!

There is much talk about the "mark" being a microchip of some sort, and I believe that this technology is probably the device that will be used, because we are all being desensitized to it now for "security" and "safety" reasons. I have seen many hand-scanners in places in the United States and am speculating now if that will be used in these latter days as spoken about in Revelation.

As we are studying the latter days, let's also examine the Old Testament and how GOD destroyed Sodom and Gomorrah for the rampant sin in these cities. We are warned that GOD will again destroy the earth for all the ungodliness that will again take place on the earth in the latter days.

We are living in these latter days that GOD has warned us about!

This time GOD will destroy the earth with fire, just as He sent down fire to destroy these two cities of sin in the Old Testament.

Sodom and Gomorrah Destroyed.

> 1 The two Angels arrived at Sodom in the evening, and Lot was sitting in the gateway of the city. When he saw them, he got up to meet them and bowed down with his face to the ground.
> 2 "My lords," he said, "please turn aside to your servant's house. You can wash your feet and spend the night and then go on your way early in the morning." "No," they answered, "we will spend the night in the square."
> 3 But he insisted so strongly that they did go with him and entered his house. He prepared a meal for them, baking bread without yeast, and they ate.
> 4 Before they had gone to bed, all the men from every part of the city of Sodom, both young and old, surrounded the house.
> 5 They called to Lot, "Where are the men who came to you tonight? Bring them out to us so that we can have sex with them."
> 6 Lot went outside to meet them and shut the door behind him
> 7 and said, "No, my friends. Don't do this wicked thing.
> 8 Look, I have two daughters who have never slept with a man. Let me bring them out to you, and you can do what you like with them. But don't do anything to these men, for they have come under the protection of my roof."
> 9 "Get out of our way," they replied. And they said, "This fellow came here as an alien, and now he wants to play the judge! We'll treat you worse than them." They kept bringing pressure on Lot and moved forward to break down the door.
> 10 But the men inside reached out and pulled Lot back into the house and shut the door.

¹¹ Then they struck the men who were at the door of the house, young and old, with blindness so that they could not find the door.

¹² The two men said to Lot, "Do you have anyone else here, sons-in-law, sons or daughters, or anyone else in the city who belongs to you? Get them out of here,

¹³ because we are going to destroy this place. The outcry to the LORD against its people is so great that He has sent us to destroy it."

¹⁴ So Lot went out and spoke to his sons-in-law, who were pledged to marry his daughters. He said, "Hurry and get out of this place, because the LORD is about to destroy the city!" But his sons-in-law thought he was joking.

¹⁵ With the coming of dawn, the Angels urged Lot, saying, "Hurry! Take your wife and your two daughters who are here, or you will be swept away when the city is punished."

¹⁶ When he hesitated, the men grasped his hand and the hands of his wife and of his two daughters and led them safely out of the city, for the LORD was merciful to them.

¹⁷ As soon as they had brought them out, one of them said, "Flee for your lives! Don't look back, and don't stop anywhere in the plain! Flee to the mountains or you will be swept away!"

¹⁸ But Lot said to them, "No, my lords, please!

¹⁹ Your servant has found favor in your eyes, and you have shown great kindness to me in sparing my life. But I can't flee to the mountains; this disaster will overtake me, and I'll die.

²⁰ Look, here is a town near enough to run to, and it is small. Let me flee to it, it is very small, isn't it? Then my life will be spared."

²¹ He said to him, "Very well, I will grant this request too; I will not overthrow the town you speak of.

²² But flee there quickly, because I cannot do anything until you reach it." (That is why the town was called Zoar.)

²³ By the time Lot reached Zoar, the sun had risen over the land.

²⁴ Then the LORD rained down burning sulfur on Sodom and Gomorrah, from the LORD out of the heavens.

²⁵ Thus He overthrew those cities and the entire plain, including all those living in the cities, and also the vegetation in the land.
²⁶ But Lot's wife looked back, and she became a pillar of salt.
²⁷ Early the next morning Abraham got up and returned to the place where he had stood before the LORD.
²⁸ He looked down toward Sodom and Gomorrah, toward all the land of the plain and he saw dense smoke rising from the land, like smoke from a furnace.
²⁹ So when GOD destroyed the cities of the plain, He remembered Abraham, and He brought Lot out of the catastrophe that overthrew the cities where Lot had lived.

Genesis 19: NIV

Lot found favor in GOD's eyes and it is my prayer that in the coming tribulations upon the earth, we will find such favor in the eyes of GOD. If we have given our life to Jesus Christ, we will be spared from this second storm of fire that will destroy the earth. If we have not, we will not find GOD's mercy and grace.

GOD kept His promise to Abraham and later Sarah gave birth to their son, the one that GOD promised through His Angels, even though in the natural Sarah and Abraham were much too old to bear a child. They named their son Issac, the one promised many, many years before he was finally conceived and born.

GOD will keep His promise to you also!

GOD is not a man that He should lie. So, don't grow tired waiting for the promises that GOD has spoken to your heart, be patient in waiting. We must remember that a day to the Lord is like a thousand years, as is quoted below.

⁸ But do not forget this one thing, dear friends: with the Lord a day is like a thousand years, and a thousand years are like a day.
⁹ The Lord is not slow in keeping His promise, as some understand slowness. He is patient with you, not wanting anyone to perish, but everyone to come to repentance.

2 Peter 3:8-9 NIV

Can you envision if you had presented a beautiful gift that you had to sacrifice much for; only to give the gift to someone you deeply loved, and have them throw the gift back into your face?

It would hurt your heart deeply, just as it has hurt the heart of GOD!

Imagine how hard it must have been to have your Son sacrificed for so many, and then to see the people turn away and not receive the gift He so freely gave.

Can you just imagine sacrificing your child?

I feel at times the heartbeat of GOD and His sorrows as He looks down on a world so calloused and broken with sin.

GOD had to destroy mankind in those cities before and He knows He will again have to destroy His creation, made in His image.

Do many not recognize the condition their souls are in? Do they not know they are wretched, poor and pitiful?

What Must Be Taught to Various Groups.

1. You must teach what is in accord with sound doctrine.
2. Teach the older men to be temperate, worthy of respect, self-controlled, and sound in faith, in love and in endurance.
3. Likewise, teach the older women to be reverent in the way they live, not to be slanderers or addicted to much wine, but to teach what is good.
4. Then they can train the younger women to love their husbands and children,
5. to be self-controlled and pure, to be busy at home, to be kind, and to be subject to their husbands, so that no one will malign the word of GOD.
6. Similarly, encourage the young men to be self-controlled.
7. In everything set them an example by doing what is good. In your teaching show integrity, seriousness,
8. and soundness of speech that cannot be condemned, so that those who oppose you may be ashamed because they have nothing bad to say about us.
9. Teach slaves to be subject to their masters in everything, to try to please them, not to talk back to them,

¹⁰ and not to steal from them, but to show that they can be fully trusted, so that in every way they will make the teaching about GOD our Savior attractive.

¹¹ For the grace of GOD that brings salvation has appeared to all men.

¹² It teaches us to say "No" to ungodliness and worldly passions, and to live self-controlled, upright and Godly lives in this present age,

¹³ while we wait for the blessed hope, the glorious appearing of our great GOD and Savior, Jesus Christ,

¹⁴ who gave Himself for us, to redeem us from all wickedness and to purify for Himself a people that are His very own; eager to do what is good.

¹⁵ These, then, are the things you should teach. Encourage and rebuke with all authority. Do not let anyone despise you.

Titus 2 NIV

My heart's cry is that they find and know the LORD Jesus and what a great price He paid to free them from their sins and bondages! Multitudes write-off what Jesus did as simply a history lesson or a type of belief system for someone else.

June 27, 2005
3:20 a.m.

My beloved,

You did well to meditate on my Word, you will learn much from the CD's and it will strengthen your spirit.

I have planted you in a good Church who is seeking me and they teach the truth of me and my WORD. It will be good to see you involved in the ministry and you will have a voice and can teach others what I teach you.

Most do not hear from me as you do, they have sin that hinders them and their walk with me.

You have been transparent before me and you are hungry for the deeper things of me. This pleased the Father's heart because you do

not wish to grow fat on my teachings, but you desire to equip others and you are a willing vessel. In time, you will be a leader and used mightily by me.

The secret thing that most of my Body does not understand is the reality that they are in a battle.

This life on earth is clouded with supernatural battles all around them. Because it is in the supernatural, they do not see and they don't realize the seriousness of it. Your enemy and their enemy are real and many think it my job to stop him from harm in their lives.

It is true that my Holy Elect, I do rebuke the devourer for their sakes. Those are the few that are sold out to me. They are obedient, they heed my voice and instructions and they give tithes and offerings to their Church.

This is the narrow road; most are on the wide road.

They must understand that I do not desire a lip service Saint; I will spit them out of my mouth. They are men pleasers and are there for the applaud of men.

I see the hearts of all and I know who are mine and who are not, they do not fool me.

You are being transformed in your heart and mind and I know the changes in you that are yet to come. You must get it deep in your spirit how much I love you and need you. You must believe in yourself and don't focus on the negative, the things in you that you are not pleased with.

You are made in my image and I will perfect your body and take off the excess weight which hinders you from believing in yourself.

You need to transform your mind from the much abuse you have suffered in order to be prepared to be strong enough to handle the new body. You will be fine and you must believe in yourself and know that I hold all your days in my hand. Losing the weight will not make you a bad person, you can handle the flesh, your spirit is strong and in control.

Go ahead and seek to replace those old images with new ones. Understand that your physical beauty was destroyed by Satan, working through Philip and your scars are painful and run deep.

Do not let the enemy of your soul continue to hold you in bondage. He uses this to attack many of my servants by keeping them in bondage.

It is not the food, all things are free to eat in moderation, but Satan being my most beautiful Angel in creation desires to triumph over my Saints and he uses their appearances, to drag them down into this bondage so he can shine in my eyes.

He is a fool to think I don't see his attempts for adoration.

My holy ones should be the most physically beautiful on the earth, but Satan has played with the minds of millions to believe they are unworthy, etc. It is just another diversion that he uses to get the focus on themselves and stay in bondage, thus rendering them ineffective in their witnessing to others.

Now you understand another tactic of the devil and you have the authority to stop the thoughts and actions that lead you to destroying your body.

Keep seeking me, my beloved and I will share with you the deeper things of me.

Shalom, my precious child.

GOD's desire for each of us is to live a life of holiness. Each person has a consciousness from GOD, and the Holy Spirit will guide those that belong to Jesus in the way they should live and dress, in all manners of respect.

We are a society that is too casual in dress and too skimpy in a lot of the fashions of today. There is nothing left to the imagination and it is not GOD's desire to see our bodies used for an unholy pleasure. I know that sounds "old fashioned," yet GOD is as old as time itself and some freedoms are just not worth it.

We should take heed and warning from the message He sent to me about our appearances and being adorned with beauty in ourselves. Beauty comes from the inside out, not the outside in.

Jesus sacrifice on the cross was for you and every person on this earth!

Many have died without receiving the gift of salvation and I pray that you do not!

There are no coincidences in life, if you are reading this book, then please know you have a destiny designed by GOD to receive Him and to live a life worthy of Him.

Won't you give your heart to Jesus?

Chapter Five

His Warnings

*G*OD has sent many warnings to His people!
We have seen many famines, earthquakes, hurricanes, tornados and the like upon the face of the earth and it seems with every year that passes by, the wickedness increases throughout the land.

We have seen terrorism on a much grander scale than ever before. People everywhere are affected by the violence and evil that is rampart on our streets and neighborhoods and many people are crying out for answers. Many are searching for the truth!

We all want to find meaning in our lives and we want to live in peace and harmony with others of the world. That is one reason we have fallen into much acceptance and we don't live with absolute values anymore.

Why is this happening?

It is because the love of most people has grown cold and wickedness permeates our society! Many people no longer have an agenda to help others, they are selfish and self-seeking. We are a society immersed in our social agenda's and busy schedules.

Read as the Scripture below describes a people in the last days.

[12] Because of the increase of wickedness, the love of most will grow cold.

Matthew 24:12 NIV

I, however, am not discouraged.

I believe there are many wonderful people who are living a pleasing and acceptable life before Jesus Christ. They are sold out and a bright witness for Him. These are not the ones that GOD is sending a warning to, but it is helpful to be reminded of the times we live in.

I know I was called to write this book to the unbeliever's hearts, to again tell them that Jesus loves them and to the believer's hearts, this book should be an encouraging one, not a correctional teaching, but a mutual edifying of each other's spirit.

As I am writing this book, the world is watching the next hurricane (Katrina) to hit the shores of Florida, Alabama, Louisiana, and Mississippi. There is much fear and speculation of the loss of homes, businesses and lives. My Church and I have been praying for the salvation of souls that might be lost in this hurricane. I am sure there are many Churches and Saints alike rising up and praying at this very hour.

Perhaps that is why I was awakened early, the morning of August 29th and these were the words that GOD spoke to me in my Spirit.

It is with much heartache that I share His words with you and I hope that you can see the heart of GOD in this next message. It was given to me perhaps minutes before Katrina hit the shores of Louisiana, Alabama and Mississippi.

August 29, 2005
4:00 a.m.

My beloved,

Many are the plans I have set before you. I will guide you in which way to walk. Many things of the Kingdom are being established right now and many will perish as I send destruction upon the land. I wish that none would perish, but they have made their choices.

They follow Baal and they mock even my very existence. They spit on my Son, Yeshua and they do not heed my warnings. My wrath is here and it starts with the cities of sin and my Churches. My Church needs to rise up in this last hour and warn the people.

I will not be silent forever!

I am Sovereign and I will not be mocked. Many say they follow me, yet they are liars and will find themselves in the Lake of Fire for all eternity.

My beloved, I have equipped you to write my words and I've given you a heart for the salvation of their souls. You do understand the deeper things of me. Many <u>play</u> church and think they are being a light for me, they are an abomination in my sight!

By their fruit you will recognize them.

Many things are happening in your life right now, it will begin to move faster as I need you to move to a higher place in me. You realize the hour in which you live and also understand that you can't be entangled with the world. You are set apart and this must be so to survive and be effective in these last days.

You have no need of worldly entertainment; it will sour your spirit and can cause you to miss the mark!

I love you with an everlasting love because you are mine; we are one!

Many will suffer, even in the midst of the storm, many will not cry out for me. Many will perish and go down to the deep, spending their eternity in Hell.

Oh, my beloved, if only my people understood how much I love them! If only they understood the depth of my love.

Yet, Satan has their eyes blinded to the truth and they live in darkness, they cannot perceive what is in front of them.

I weep as they scream and go into the deep, never to rejoice and praise me.

Shalom, my beloved Servant,
in you I am well pleased.

The heart of GOD is so fragile, yet gentle and strong. His love for us is so incomprehensible that we can oftentimes find it hard to believe that He is dependent on us to love Him in return.

GOD is love, the author of love and the finisher of love. GOD only disciplines us because He loves us so much and He wants what is best for us, for all of mankind.

As the devastation from Katrina is now being felt throughout Louisiana, Alabama, Mississippi, Florida and other parts of America, it saddens me to see the loss of life, the suffering of people both far and wide.

I am witnessing many, many good people coming out of their comfort zones to aid these homeless thousands.

I am proud to live in Texas and to see first-hand all the outpouring of love demonstrated by my fellow Texans in this drastic time of need.

My heart has been heavy this past week and I have been overcome with darkness, sleepless nights and much anxiety. I know my Lord had to discipline the people and I feel so helpless at times. I am sure that GOD is suffering watching so many in despair. Just as a parent, we dislike the discipline we inflict on our own children, it is the same with GOD.

It was never GOD's intention to punish us or to have our lives be difficult; yet His created Angel Lucifer, turned into the devil through a prideful and haughty spirit, which is known as Satan, and thus changed the course of history, not only for us, but for all living creatures.

> [7] "And there was war in heaven. Michael and His Angels fought against the dragon, and the dragon and his Angels fought back.
> [8] But he was not strong enough, and they lost their place in heaven.
> [9] The great dragon was hurled down, that ancient serpent called the devil, or Satan, who leads the whole world astray. He was hurled to the earth, and his Angels with him.
> [10] Then I heard a loud voice in heaven say: Now have come the salvation and the power and the kingdom of our GOD, and the authority of His Christ. For the accuser of our brothers, who accuses them before our GOD day and night, has been hurled down.
> [11] They overcame him by the blood of the Lamb and by the word of their testimony; they did not love their lives so much as to shrink from death.
> [12] Therefore rejoice you heavens and you who dwell in them! But woe to the earth and the sea, because the devil has gone

down to you! He is filled with fury, because he knows that his time is short."

Revelation 12:7-12 NIV

I find myself asking, what is the future for our children and our children's children?

Perhaps you are asking yourself that same question. I also have a burning question in me, which is, when will the end come?

When will Jesus Christ return for His bride?

I am always looking for HIM and hoping that there is still enough time to get this book out and the next one I am also writing.

I believe as we get closer to His return for all His Holy ones, we will suffer more violence, more pestilence, more famines, and more natural disasters than ever before.

As I wrote some of the text yesterday, I was again awakened by GOD and given this next message. There is really no way to preface it, but to just let it speak for itself.

As you can see from the date, it was written just two days after the devastating hurricane named Katrina.

August 31, 2005
4:05 a.m.

My beloved,

I have caused much destruction on the earth. Some are calling forth my name, yet once they are comforted, they quickly forget me.

I Am that I Am.

I send the winds and rains, my wrath is being poured out on a wicked generation who dismisses me, I will not tolerate the wickedness as it is abounding on the earth.

I see many of my Saints growing weary in the battles before them. They must take time to dwell in my presence to let the oil of joy run over them and to seek me and cling to my promises.

I am the same and I do not change!

As the wickedness so increases on the land, so will my judgments.

If people would humble themselves and turn from their wickedness and the way they are living, I would call the Angels together and have them hold back the winds of destruction.

I would heal the land and wipe the tears away from their eyes.

That is why my gospel must be preached, so many are perishing.

The Holy Spirit has been poured out like a drink offering and in my grace and mercy; I have sent Him into the whole world to speak to the multitudes. If only they would listen and turn their hearts toward me. I am waiting to send my Son, Yeshua to the Earth, until all has been accomplished.

I know my sheep are growing weary in the battle. Encourage them not to give up, or I will not be pleased with them, they must endure hardships a little longer.

Trust in me and don't look to the right or the left, you are my messenger sent into the wilderness crying out for their salvation. You will be greatly rewarded, as will all my precious Saints who have not forsaken their first love and they still call on me for fellowship.

It is one thing to have the worship and adoration of my Angels, it is quite another to have my precious people, created in my image, to worship me.

It pleases the heart of the Father and He delights in the praises of a pure heart. Like any earthly Father, He longs to give good gifts to His children.

I know many have questions about my character and if I claim to love the people, why do I bring harm and destruction on them?

Because I am also a jealous GOD; a consuming fire, but I do not desire your adoration simply for my pleasure. If only you understood the depth and vastness of my love for all mankind and how much I want to bless you.

I cannot bless you and dwell with you, if you live in sin and darkness.

My spirit cannot dwell in the wicked hearts!

I offer a better way, I offer complete forgiveness, healing, wholeness, restoration, healing of your bodies and your souls, if only you would lay down your wicked lifestyles and put off your old habits and seek me.

You must trade in your old way of life to really live and I offer all those things to a hurting world.

My wrath is being poured out very small right now, it is only the beginning!

I will equip my Saints to go to you and minister to your hurting hearts. My Saints are doing battle in the spiritual world right now and if I were to call them all home now, there would be no restraints on the earth. The wickedness would abound and seeking me will be much harder.

The time to repent is now, before more destruction comes upon the earth!

I will not leave my Saints to suffer forever, but will call them home at my appointed time.

Many suffer and are persecuted right now for the sake of sharing my gospel; they have surrendered their all in living their lives subjected to me. They will be greatly rewarded and will sit around my throne, with the twenty-four elders who worship me continually.

So heed my words and seek me while my mercy knows no end.

There is an appointed time set for the final battle and my Saints will rule and reign with me. Just as a commander in an army seeks the best, my Saints are being perfected to not fail me at the final hour.

Many are learning to lay down everything in their lives. Some have sacrificed their families who wouldn't journey with them; some have forsaken mother and father, some their own children for the calling I have placed on them.

They will be rewarded and they understand that multitudes are dying without a Savior.

My Saints are being sent out in the battle to do war against Satan and his demons, to bring the truth to a hurting and dying world.

Many do not understand my people, they are peculiar to the world, they are not of the world, and have sacrificed much to serve me. They are not bound by the material things of life, because they know all possessions are futile to treasure.

It is time to realize the hour in which mankind lives and to prepare your hearts for the coming of my Son, Yeshua. He will come in the clouds. My sign will appear in the Heavens, a brightness you have never seen before and all will see His entry from the Heavens to Earth.

Many will leap to their own death when they see Him and men's hearts will fail them at the appearing of Jesus.

But my Saints who are prepared and have fought the battles will rejoice.

The lukewarm of my Church will suddenly realize their condition and be filled with sorrow.

My Saints must press in right now and take most seriously the call they have on their life. There is much to do and while they sit on the fence of indecision, people are perishing.

You have been strategically placed in your workplace or home to make a difference. Many are not in their armor and doing battle for me.

Many hear my call, the tug on their hearts. I speak to them, but they are consumed with the cares and worries of their own life. This is the tactic of the devil to keep my people in constant struggles and strife, so they are most ineffective in their lives and find no room to tell the world about Jesus Christ, who sacrificed it all to save them from the wrath and the judgments.

I have much to say about the judgments. I will reveal it at a later writing.

Warn the people my beloved, and share this message so that many souls will be saved from this earth and will live in eternity with the Saints to worship me.

There will be joy unending and all your sufferings now cannot even be compared to the future glory I have for my Saints. Endure till the end and keep calling out to the lost generation.

My words are to be heard from afar, seek me and you will find me.

Shalom, my beloved, till we meet again.

As you can see from the preceding message of GOD, He is desperate to reach the lost!

His discipline has been most harsh and some will question that GOD caused the hurricanes and will blame the devil for this suffering and destruction! As I write this book, many Preachers are blaming the devil for this destruction already.

I will stand in dispute of them!

GOD is in control of His universe that He created. It is absurd to me to think that GOD Almighty cannot control the devil?

Of course He can, and He does!

GOD will oftentimes allow Satan to tempt us and He will often take His hand of protection from us; however, this wrath was poured out by GOD himself!

He does control the winds, and the weather and we cannot even begin to always understand the ways of the LORD, because His ways are higher than our ways.

I would not want to sacrifice my life into the hands of a GOD, who is not in control, would you?

If He is GOD, the GOD of Abraham, Issac and Jacob, He is the GOD that I serve!

> [1] Praise the LORD, O my soul. O LORD my God, you are very great; you are clothed with splendor and majesty.
> [2] He wraps Himself in light as with a garment; He stretches out the heavens like a tent,
> [3] and lays the beams of His upper chambers on their waters. He makes the clouds His chariot and rides on the wings of the wind.
> [4] He makes winds His messengers, flames of fire His servants.
> [5] He set the earth on its foundations; it can never be moved.
> [6] You covered it with the deep as with a garment; the waters stood above the mountains.
> [7] But at your rebuke the waters fled, at the sound of your thunder they took to flight;
> [8] they flowed over the mountains, they went down into the valleys, to the place you assigned for them.
> [9] You set a boundary they cannot cross; never again will they cover the earth.
> [10] He makes springs pour water into the ravines; it flows between the mountains.

11. They give water to all the beasts of the field; the wild donkeys quench their thirst.
12. The birds of the air nest by the waters; they sing among the branches.
13. He waters the mountains from His upper chambers; the earth is satisfied by the fruit of His work.
14. He makes grass grow for the cattle, and plants for man to cultivate bringing forth food from the earth:
15. wine that gladdens the heart of man, oil to make his face shine, and bread that sustains his heart.
16. The trees of the LORD are well watered, the cedars of Lebanon that He planted.
17. There the birds make their nests; the stork has its home in the pine trees.
18. The high mountains belong to the wild goats; the crags are a refuge for the coneys.
19. The moon marks off the seasons, and the sun knows when to go down.
20. You bring darkness; it becomes night, and all the beasts of the forest prowl.
21. The lions roar for their prey and seek their food from God.
22. The sun rises, and they steal away; they return and lie down in their dens.
23. Then man goes out to his work, to his labor until evening.
24. How many are your works, O LORD! In wisdom you made them all; the earth is full of your creatures.
25. There is the sea, vast and spacious, teeming with creatures beyond number, living things both large and small.
26. There the ships go to and fro, and the leviathan, which you formed to frolic there.
27. These all look to you to give them their food at the proper time.
28. When you give it to them, they gather it up; when you open your hand, they are satisfied with good things.
29. When you hide your face, they are terrified; when you take away their breath, they die and return to the dust.
30. When you send your Spirit, they are created, and you renew the face of the earth.

³¹ May the Glory of the LORD endure forever; may the LORD rejoice in His works,
³² He who looks at the earth, and it trembles, who touches the mountains, and they smoke.
³³ I will sing to the LORD all my life; I will sing praise to my God as long as I live.
³⁴ May my meditation be pleasing to Him, as I rejoice in the LORD.
³⁵ But may sinners vanish from the earth and the wicked be no more. Praise the LORD, O my soul. Praise the LORD.

Psalm 104 NIV

Just as the Psalmist praised GOD so long ago, I too find many, many wonderful works of my Father to praise Him for daily. It only takes a moment of time spent in nature to see His marvelous works.

Sadly, these days will end and those who reject His truth will spend their eternity in Hell. For the Saints of GOD, those who belong to the LORD, our eternity will be in Heaven!

It is for the unbeliever's heart that GOD warns us about the latter days and how to read the signs of the times. He is trying to encourage His people to hold on until the end, and He is sending a wake-up call to the lost.

Which group do you belong to?

The earth's time is quickly running out and we must recognize the condition of our spiritual life, before Jesus returns for His bride.

GOD knew that in the latter days there would be many who would be preaching a false doctrine and perverting the ways of the LORD Almighty. That is why He has given us this warning.

A Tree and Its Fruit.

¹⁵ "Watch out for false prophets. They come to you in sheep's clothing, but inwardly they are ferocious wolves.
¹⁶ By their fruit you will recognize them. Do people pick grapes from thorn bushes, or figs from thistles?
¹⁷ Likewise every good tree bears good fruit, but a bad tree bears bad fruit.

18 A good tree cannot bear bad fruit, and a bad tree cannot bear good fruit.
19 Every tree that does not bear good fruit is cut down and thrown into the fire.
20 Thus, by their fruit you will recognize them."
21 "Not everyone who says to me, 'Lord, Lord,' will enter the kingdom of heaven, but only he who does the will of my Father who is in heaven.
22 Many will say to me on that day, 'Lord, Lord, did we not prophesy in your name and in your name drive out demons and perform many miracles?'
23 Then I will tell them plainly, 'I never knew you. Away from me, you evildoers!'"

The Wise and Foolish Builders.

24 "Therefore everyone who hears these words of mine and puts them into practice is like a wise man who built his house on the rock.
25 The rain came down, the streams rose, and the winds blew and beat against that house; yet it did not fall, because it had its foundation on the rock.
26 But everyone who hears these words of mine and does not put them into practice is like a foolish man who built his house on sand.
27 The rain came down, the streams rose, and the winds blew and beat against that house, and it fell with a great crash."
28 When Jesus had finished saying these things, the crowds were amazed at His teaching;
29 because He taught as one who had authority, and not as their teachers of the law.

Matthew 7:13-29 NIV

Jesus still teaches us with His great authority and many are listening to His voice crying out to a nation and a world that needs to repent and turn to Him for their salvation!

He does not offer us an eternity full of heartache, but one full of peace. An eternity spent in Heaven praising Him, and GOD the Father!

We can all spend our eternity in a beautiful place singing with the Angels, if we will surrender our hearts to Jesus Christ!

GOD is a mighty and just GOD. He is much more than just love, He is Righteousness, the Prince of Peace and He is also Sovereign.

What we reap on this earth, is what we will sow on this earth, as well as our eternal destination!

September 2, 2005
6:05 a.m.

My beloved,

I see people suffering and crying out to me. My Saints are rising up and showing my love to others in need.

People are being reminded what is really important and are reaching out.

Tell my people I love them and whatever they give to those in need will be returned back to them. I will supply their needs and I will equip my people to be a light to those who have now turned their hearts to me! Many are ripe to hear my gospel. The workers need to go into the fields, the harvest is ripe.

It saddens me that I must go to great measures to get people to remember what is precious in life and for them to lay down their idols. I will take care of my people whom I created, they only need to ask in my Son's name, Jesus and I will give it to them.

The principle of reaping and sowing is very real and one only has to look to find someone in need to help.

People need to love each other with an open heart and do not get bitter at the trials you are facing. Much good will come from this destruction.

The City can start fresh and rebuild it, my wish is they not return to their wicked ways, but to return with a changed heart and being grateful for their very lives, something most take for granted.

I love my people with an everlasting love. I rebuke and correct those I love and you must tell them how much I love them!

Shalom, my beloved.

As we've just read above, GOD dealt with the City of New Orleans harshly to get their attention to the rampant sin in their lives and He has also given them the ability to rebuild their City. My prayer is that the citizens of that great City search their hearts and find the love of Jesus Christ and not be bitter, but be thankful that He spared so many people's lives.

There are miracles everywhere that demonstrate GOD's abundant provisions for so many and they serve as a testimony to the rest of the world of what is really important. Life is important, its value is far-reaching and many are being reminded of that. Possessions can be replaced, but our families are here for only a season, and our time is ever short!

Just as in the Old Testament, GOD freed His people, the Israelites, from the slavery of the Egyptians. Yet, when they disobeyed Him in the wilderness, He caused them to wander around for forty years, until the first generation had died, then He led them, through the leadership of Joshua, to the Promised Land. Moses wasn't even allowed to enter it, but to only see it from afar. Moses was punished because of the disobedience of the people. GOD dealt harshly with that generation, but He also provided their every need.

Even though Moses was not permitted to enter into the Promised Land, GOD marked Moses as being the meekest man on earth. He was so important even the devil fought with the Archangel Michael over his dead body.

> 9 But even the Archangel Michael, when he was disputing with the devil about the body of Moses, did not dare to bring a slanderous accusation against him, but said, "The Lord rebuke you!"
>
> Jude 1:9 NIV

Do Not Forget the LORD.

> [1] Be careful to follow every command I am giving you today, so that you may live and increase and may enter and possess the land that the LORD promised on oath to your forefathers.
> [2] Remember how the LORD your GOD led you all the way in the desert these forty years, to humble you and to test you in order to know what was in your heart, whether or not you would keep His commands.
> [3] He humbled you, causing you to hunger and then feeding you with manna, which neither you nor your fathers had known, to teach you that man does not live on bread alone but on every word that comes from the mouth of the LORD.
> [4] Your clothes did not wear out and your feet did not swell during these forty years.
> [5] Know then in your heart that as a man disciplines his son, so the LORD your GOD disciplines you.
> [6] Observe the commands of the LORD your GOD, walking in His ways and revering Him.
> [7] For the LORD your GOD is bringing you into a good land, a land with streams and pools of water, with springs flowing in the valleys and hills;
> [8] a land with wheat and barley, vines and fig trees, pomegranates, olive oil and honey;
> [9] a land where bread will not be scarce and you will lack nothing; a land where the rocks are iron and you can dig copper out of the hills.
> [10] When you have eaten and are satisfied, praise the LORD your GOD for the good land He has given you.
> [11] Be careful that you do not forget the LORD your GOD, failing to observe His commands, His laws and His decrees that I am giving you this day.
> [12] Otherwise, when you eat and are satisfied, when you build fine houses and settle down,
> [13] and when your herds and flocks grow large and your silver and gold increase and all you have is multiplied,

14 then your heart will become proud and you will forget the LORD your GOD, who brought you out of Egypt, out of the land of slavery.
15 He led you through the vast and dreadful desert, that thirsty and waterless land, with its venomous snakes and scorpions. He brought you water out of hard rock.
16 He gave you manna to eat in the desert, something your fathers had never known, to humble and to test you so that in the end it might go well with you.
17 You may say to yourself, "My power and the strength of my hands have produced this wealth for me."
18 But remember the LORD your GOD, for it is He who gives you the ability to produce wealth, and so confirms His covenant, which He swore to your forefathers, as it is today.
19 If you ever forget the LORD your GOD and follow other Gods and worship and bow down to them, I testify against you today that you will surely be destroyed.
20 Like the nations the LORD destroyed before you, so you will be destroyed for not obeying the LORD your GOD.

Deuteronomy 8 NIV

GOD has not changed!

He is still in control and He is warning a people, once again, of their disobedience and what lies ahead for them. I believe all these "natural" disasters that keep pouring out wrath on our world are caused by the Hand of GOD and they will increase until Jesus comes for His bride.

Then, He will one day cause every knee to bow and every tongue to confess that HE is Lord.

1 If you have any encouragement from being united with Christ, if any comfort from His love, if any fellowship with the Spirit, if any tenderness and compassion,
2 then make my joy complete by being like-minded, having the same love, being one in spirit and purpose.
3 Do nothing out of selfish ambition or vain conceit, but in humility consider others better than yourselves.

⁴Each of you should look not only to your own interests, but also to the interests of others.

⁵Your attitude should be the same as that of Christ Jesus.

⁶Who, being in very nature GOD, did not consider equality with GOD something to be grasped,

⁷but made Himself nothing, taking the very nature of a servant, being made in human likeness.

⁸And being found in appearance as a man, He humbled Himself and became obedient to death, even death on a cross!

⁹Therefore GOD exalted Him to the highest place and gave Him the name that is above every name,

¹⁰that at the name of Jesus every knee should bow, in heaven and on earth and under the earth,

¹¹and every tongue confess that Jesus Christ is Lord, to the glory of GOD the Father.

¹²Therefore, my dear friends, as you have always obeyed, not only in my presence, but now much more in my absence, continue to work out your salvation with fear and trembling,

¹³for it is GOD who works in you to will and to act according to His good purpose.

Philippians 2:1-13 NIV

It is such a hard thing to realize that GOD does love us when we are experiencing His wrath on us. It is difficult to understand the ways of GOD and I will be the first to admit that as much as I love Him, it is hard to endure His punishments.

I understand that we all need to be corrected and it is for our own good, but no discipline is pleasing at the time, but afterwards we can always look back on our lives and see the good it did for us.

I am so saddened by the destruction and the sufferings of the people that survived Katrina. It is horrific to watch the people suffer so much.

There are no adequate words to describe how helpless countless thousands of us felt watching our fellow human beings suffering so much and we didn't have the means to get to them to help. I can only imagine it felt like an eternity before help arrived.

Perhaps that is the message GOD is trying to tell us. As bad as this suffering is, it is nothing compared to the eternal suffering in Hell forever.

"Oh, GOD, please show us your mercy and your grace once more so that we can strive to live a life pleasing and Holy unto you!

On behalf of all those suffering Lord, hear my prayers for them and supernaturally grant them peace, and all things they need at this time.

In Jesus Name, I pray. Amen."

Please know that in no way do I wish to exalt myself at any level, I am only heeding the calling on my life. I would be most inadequate to fill the pages of your mind with words that would convince your heart to change.

No, it is by the Holy Spirit dwelling in me, through Christ Jesus, that I am able to pencil these words for you.

I find in the text below that we are living in the words of this book of the Bible, Matthew 24 which instructs us to watch for the signs of the end of the age.

> [1] Jesus left the temple and was walking away when His disciples came up to Him to call His attention to its buildings.
> [2] "Do you see all these things?" He asked. "I tell you the truth, not one stone here will be left on another; every one will be thrown down."
> [3] As Jesus was sitting on the Mount of Olives, the disciples came to Him privately. "Tell us," they said, "when will this happen, and what will be the sign of your coming and of the end of the age?"
> [4] Jesus answered: "Watch out that no one deceives you.
> [5] For many will come in my name, claiming, 'I am the Christ,' and will deceive many.
> [6] You will hear of wars and rumors of wars, but see to it that you are not alarmed. Such things must happen, but the end is still to come.
> [7] Nation will rise against nation, and kingdom against kingdom. There will be famines and earthquakes in various places.

⁸ All these are the beginning of birth pains."

⁹ "Then you will be handed over to be persecuted and put to death, and you will be hated by all nations because of me.

¹⁰ At that time many will turn away from the faith and will betray and hate each other,

¹¹ and many false prophets will appear and deceive many people.

¹² Because of the increase of wickedness, the love of most will grow cold,

¹³ but he who stands firm to the end will be saved.

¹⁴ And this gospel of the kingdom will be preached in the whole world as a testimony to all nations, and then the end will come."

¹⁵ "So when you see standing in the holy place 'the abomination that causes desolation,' spoken of through the prophet Daniel, let the reader understand,

¹⁶ then let those who are in Judea flee to the mountains.

¹⁷ Let no one on the roof of his house go down to take anything out of the house.

¹⁸ Let no one in the field go back to get his cloak.

¹⁹ How dreadful it will be in those days for pregnant women and nursing mothers!

²⁰ Pray that your flight will not take place in winter or on the Sabbath.

²¹ For then there will be great distress, unequaled from the beginning of the world until now and never to be equaled again.

²² If those days had not been cut short, no one would survive, but for the sake of the elect those days will be shortened.

²³ At that time if anyone says to you, 'Look, here is the Christ!' or, 'There He is!' do not believe it.

²⁴ For false Christ's and false prophets will appear and perform great signs and miracles to deceive even the elect, if that were possible.

²⁵ See, I have told you ahead of time."

²⁶ "So if anyone tells you, 'There He is, out in the desert,' do not go out; or, 'Here He is, in the inner rooms,' do not believe it.

²⁷ For as lightning that comes from the east is visible even in the west, so will be the coming of the Son of Man.

²⁸ Wherever there is a carcass, there the vultures will gather."

²⁹ "Immediately after the distress of those days the sun will be darkened, and the moon will not give its light; the stars will fall from the sky, and the heavenly bodies will be shaken."

³⁰ "At that time the sign of the Son of Man will appear in the sky, and all the nations of the earth will mourn. They will see the Son of Man coming on the clouds of the sky, with power and great glory.

³¹ And He will send His Angels with a loud trumpet call, and they will gather His elect from the four winds, from one end of the heavens to the other."

³² "Now learn this lesson from the fig tree: As soon as its twigs get tender and its leaves come out, you know that summer is near.

³³ Even so, when you see all these things, you know that it is near, right at the door.

³⁴ I tell you the truth; this generation will certainly not pass away until all these things have happened.

³⁵ Heaven and earth will pass away, but my words will never pass away."

³⁶ "No one knows about that day or hour, not even the Angels in Heaven, nor the Son, but only the Father."

³⁷ "As it was in the days of Noah, so it will be at the coming of the Son of Man.

³⁸ For in the days before the flood, people were eating and drinking, marrying and giving in marriage, up to the day Noah entered the ark;

³⁹ and they knew nothing about what would happen until the flood came and took them all away. That is how it will be at the coming of the Son of Man.

⁴⁰ Two men will be in the field; one will be taken and the other left.

⁴¹ Two women will be grinding with a hand mill; one will be taken and the other left."

⁴² "Therefore keep watch, because you do not know on what day your Lord will come."

⁴³ "But understand this: If the owner of the house had known at what time of night the thief was coming, he would have kept watch and would not have let his house be broken into.

⁴⁴ So you also must be ready, because the Son of Man will come at an hour when you do not expect Him."
⁴⁵ "Who then is the faithful and wise servant, whom the master has put in charge of the servants in his household to give them their food at the proper time?
⁴⁶ It will be good for that servant whose master finds him doing so when He returns.
⁴⁷ I tell you the truth; He will put him in charge of all his possessions.
⁴⁸ But suppose that servant is wicked and says to himself, 'My master is staying away a long time,'
⁴⁹ and he then begins to beat his fellow servants and to eat and drink with drunkards.
⁵⁰ The master of that servant will come on a day when he does not expect him and at an hour he is not aware of.
⁵¹ He will cut him to pieces and assign him a place with the hypocrites, where there will be weeping and gnashing of teeth."

Matthew 24 NIV

Weeping and gnashing of teeth is a term that runs throughout the Bible when describing Hell.

For all of eternity, those whose destinies are in Hell will forever be weeping, never being consoled and the gnashing of teeth describes demons that will actually be tearing away at your flesh.

You will burn, but never burn up.

I cannot imagine the horrors of that place, nor do I want to do anything in my life to cause you, my loved ones, or myself, to stumble and end up for all of eternity in Hell.

I can't say this strongly enough, I don't want YOU to ever go there!

This book was written for the multitudes who do not know Jesus Christ as their Savior. It was not for my good pleasure to write it, but for the saving of many souls into the Kingdom of GOD.

I am simply the messenger and I cannot change the message, no matter how hard it is for me to write it.

This book was not written solely for your comfort, but for your spirit and your life to be changed!

Yes, GOD does speak quietly to me and there is much responsibility that goes with being a vessel for GOD to work through.

While we are experiencing the warnings from GOD, let's continue reading and examining His words to us from the message below. It was written some months ago and it was preparing me for the time that is at hand.

March 21, 2005
4:30 a.m.

My beloved,

Do not grow weary, you are in my hands and I will equip you for every good work.

You are a faithful and mighty vessel I am able to move through. Your obedience is pleasing to me. Keep teaching my ways to your daughter, she is growing in grace and beauty and her spirit is strong.

She will seek me and serve me all the days of her life. The river of peace runs deep in her life, she is wise beyond her years. She will accomplish much for me in these last days.

People are perishing; they are dying in their sins without a Savior. Warn the people that their time is short and that I come as a thief in the night. Many are looking for my return, yet they stand unforgiven and unrepentant, they use my grace as a license to continue in their sins.

They shall have no part in the marriage supper of the Lamb.

My spirit cannot be tempted with darkness!

I am Holy and of the Light, no darkness can stand in my sight.

Just as the people go to great lengths for their earthly marriages, they put little effort in the heavenly marriage with my Son, Yeshua.

This should not be so! I am about to spit them out of my mouth.

I will not contend with them for all eternity, but will do away with them into the fiery furnace which I have warned them about. Many think it is not real.

Hell is as real as Heaven and many will go there with the Angels I have held there in chains awaiting for the final hour where I will judge the whole world, none will escape my judgment.

Many will fall under my wrath never to stand before me again. But my righteous, they live by faith, their lives in quiet submission to me; they will dwell in the light for all eternity.

There is no sickness in Heaven, only rejoicing with the Angels. There is not night, there is a constant flow of love, peace, joy and happiness such as the world has never seen or known. There will be no jealousies; no contention among everyone, for only the pure in heart will see GOD.

That is why you suffer unto perfection on earth, to set you worthy to sit around the throne of GOD. I cannot be swayed with evil. I have given the warning not to sin.

People need to heed my warnings for as in the days of Noah, people were not convinced though Noah preached his heart out. In the days of Lot, he also was not heard because of their unbelief.

But this one thing I count you worthy, keep warning and preaching my Word!

Though their hearts are hardened and their eyes blinded by the truth, keep warning so it may go well with you and their blood will not be on your hands. All things great and small will I place in your hands.

You do well to serve me. Keep writing and warning the people, you have found your calling and I will use and equip you in many ways.

My beloved, I see your surrendered heart, you are loving those who are stubborn and not seeking me. Keep encouraging and speaking my words over the faithless, though they have no part in the heavenly city, lest they turn from their wickedness.

My spirit is being poured out as a drink offering among the multitudes. I long to keep them from the fiery furnace of Hell. They were not designed for such a place! But it is their decision, that is why I've given each one their own "free will" and I cause them not to stumble.

The snare of sin has caused many to be led astray. My beloved, warn the people this should not be so.

Shalom, my precious child in whom I'm well pleased.

As if there aren't enough warnings already written in what we have read so far, let's also explore this warning from the New Testament.

Warnings from Israel's History.

> ¹ For I do not want you to be ignorant of the fact, brothers, that our forefathers were all under the cloud and that they all passed through the sea.
> ² They were all baptized into Moses in the cloud and in the sea.
> ³ They all ate the same spiritual food,
> ⁴ and drank the same spiritual drink; for they drank from the spiritual rock that accompanied them, and that rock was Christ.
> ⁵ Nevertheless, GOD was not pleased with most of them; their bodies were scattered over the desert.
> ⁶ Now these things occurred as examples to keep us from setting our hearts on evil things as they did.
> ⁷ Do not be idolaters, as some of them were; as it is written: "The people sat down to eat and drink and got up to indulge in pagan revelry."
> ⁸ We should not commit sexual immorality, as some of them did, and in one day twenty-three thousand of them died.
> ⁹ We should not test the Lord, as some of them did, and were killed by snakes.
> ¹⁰ And do not grumble, as some of them did, and were killed by the destroying Angel.
> ¹¹ These things happened to them as examples and were written down as warnings for us, on whom the fulfillment of the ages has come.
> ¹² So, if you think you are standing firm, be careful that you don't fall!
> ¹³ No temptation has seized you except what is common to man. And GOD is faithful; He will not let you be tempted beyond what you can bear. But when you are tempted, He will also provide a way out so that you can stand up under it.
> ¹⁴ Therefore, my dear friends, flee from idolatry.
> ¹⁵ I speak to sensible people; judge for yourselves what I say.

¹⁶ Is not the cup of thanksgiving for which we give thanks a participation in the blood of Christ? And is not the bread that we break a participation in the body of Christ?

¹⁷ Because there is one loaf, we, who are many, are one body, for we all partake of the one loaf.

¹⁸ Consider the people of Israel: Do not those who eat the sacrifices participate in the altar?

¹⁹ Do I mean then that a sacrifice offered to an idol is anything, or that an idol is anything?

²⁰ No, but the sacrifices of pagans are offered to demons, not to GOD, and I do not want you to be participants with demons.

²¹ You cannot drink the cup of the Lord and the cup of demons too; you cannot have a part in both the Lord's table and the table of demons.

²² Are we trying to arouse the Lord's jealousy? Are we stronger than He?

²³ "Everything is permissible," but not everything is beneficial. "Everything is permissible," but not everything is constructive.

²⁴ Nobody should seek his own good, but the good of others.

²⁵ Eat anything sold in the meat market without raising questions of conscience,

²⁶ for, "The earth is the Lord's, and everything in it."

²⁷ If some unbeliever invites you to a meal and you want to go, eat whatever is put before you without raising questions of conscience.

²⁸ But if anyone says to you, "This has been offered in sacrifice," then do not eat it, both for the sake of the man who told you and for conscience' sake,

²⁹ the other man's conscience, I mean, not yours. For why should my freedom be judged by another's conscience?

³⁰ If I take part in the meal with thankfulness, why am I denounced because of something I thank GOD for?

³¹ So whether you eat or drink or whatever you do, do it all for the glory of GOD.

³² Do not cause anyone to stumble, whether Jews, Greeks or the Church of GOD,

> ³³ even as I try to please everybody in every way. For I am not seeking my own good, but the good of many, so that they may be saved.
>
> 1 Corinthians 10 NIV

GOD's Words are so consistent throughout the entire Bible. Every word, every chapter came from the same source, the Holy Spirit of GOD Almighty, through His Son, Jesus Christ. This book also comes to you from the same source and I pray that you will fellowship with Jesus Christ as you have never before.

> ¹⁶ All Scripture is GOD-breathed and is useful for teaching, rebuking, correcting and training in righteousness,
> ¹⁷ so that the man of GOD may be thoroughly equipped for every good work.
>
> 2 Timothy 3:16-17 NIV

I pray you search long, wide, deep, and high for His voice to speak to You.

Keep seeking and He will keep speaking!

His warnings are real, as we've just read a sample of above. I trust you can find many more examples throughout the Bible, if only you will open it up and seek to find the truth.

Ask, Seek, Knock.

> ⁷ "Ask and it will be given to you; seek and you will find; knock and the door will be opened to you.
> ⁸ For everyone who asks receives; he who seeks finds; and to him who knocks, the door will be opened."
> ⁹ "Which of you, if his son asks for bread, will give him a stone?
> ¹⁰ Or if he asks for a fish, will give him a snake?
> ¹¹ If you, then, though you are evil, know how to give good gifts to your children, how much more will your Father in heaven give good gifts to those who ask him!

¹² So in everything, do to others what you would have them do to you, for this sums up the Law and the Prophets."

Matthew 7:7-12 NIV

Seek and you shall find! Knock and the door will be opened for you to receive Jesus Christ into your heart.

February 26, 2005
Friday a.m.

My beloved,

Write these words and so be filled with the Holy Spirit. I am coming in the clouds and all will see me, I will not delay.

There is still time for you to complete the tasks I have at hand for you to fulfill from the beginning of time. I brought you forth for such a time as this. I needed your bold warring spirit in these last days.

Paul served me well in the early days, you will serve me well in this last day. This is why you have been set apart. Do not despise the quiet times, though they seem lonely, you will understand later where I take you before the multitudes. You are in a training ground so you will not fail me at the final times. I will sustain you. Stay in obedience, keep up the courage, keep the joy in your heart. Many see and ponder in their heart the light you are shining into the darkness around you.

Your reward will be great. Keep up the good fight, you are not alone. As you sleep, I am there; as you work, I am there. You are never alone because you are pure in heart and you fear me and continue to serve me.

I enjoy these times alone with you. I am a jealous GOD and although I see over all mankind, you sacrifice and seek me.

Oh, how I would bless the multitudes and carry their burdens if they would only seek me as you do, but they are pre-occupied with the very life I have given them.

My spirit will not contend with them forever.

They will see my wrath in their lifetime and as you grow in obedience to me, I will show you the secret things you long to know.

Encourage one another and continue to seek me and do good for all those you meet; not just those in the faith.

Peace I leave with you.
Shalom.

Once you receive Jesus Christ into your heart, you are then ready to dwell with Him in Heaven for your eternity. Oh, how wonderful it will be to see our sweet Savior Jesus, face to face!

I can only imagine, as feelings well up inside of me now and bring me such exhilaration and joy. Tears stain my face and burn my eyes as I envision walking on the streets of gold with my brothers and sisters in Christ Jesus.

Let's walk together to the next chapter and see what GOD has in store for us in the New Jerusalem, the Heavenly City!

Chapter Six

The Heavenly City

> [1] "Do not let your hearts be troubled. Trust in GOD; trust also in me.
> [2] In my Father's house are many rooms; if it were not so, I would have told you. I am going there to prepare a place for you.
> [3] And if I go and prepare a place for you, I will come back and take you to be with me that you also may be where I am.
> [4] You know the way to the place where I am going."
>
> John 14:1-4 NIV

The preceding scriptures should be one of encouragement that Jesus Christ has provided both the gateway to Heaven and the place in Heaven for us to dwell with Him for all eternity.

He will never leave or forsake His children, and as the Scriptures attest to, He has even provided us with our heavenly dwelling.

The Narrow and Wide Gates.

> [13] "Enter through the narrow gate. For wide is the gate and broad is the road that leads to destruction, and many enter through it.
> [14] But small is the gate and narrow the road that leads to life and only a few find it."
>
> Matthew 7:13-14 NIV

Jesus is speaking of Himself as the doorway to Heaven and to access Heaven, you must accept Him as your Lord and Savior, if you want to live for all eternity in Heaven.

September 9, 2005
4:30 a.m.

My beloved,

Good morning my Servant. You do well to be obedient and write my words to warn my people of my soon return for my bride. Many are adorning themselves now with the WORD of the truth and many are seeking me. It is sad that in the adversities of life, that is when people call out to me. Many wait until they have received by their human hands to fix their problems; yet when they realize their wickedness they call out for my deliverance and for miracles to show up for them.

I am not a magic Jeannie in a bottle. I have a heart for all mankind and I love each person the same, there is no difference with me.

I do not change like the shifting shadows and I am a Man of my WORD.

There will be much rejoicing in Heaven, as you see those you love!

Blessed are the families that will find each other in the New Jerusalem and can dwell together for all eternity. They will be full of peace and joy, overflowing with love from a full heart.

I will wipe the tears from those who will mourn over their loved one who will be judged and cast into the Lake of Fire. I will comfort those who mourn.

They will realize how truly narrow the road of life is and wide is the path many took to their own demise.

I have sent my people into the world to serve as a light and a hope in this dark world. Many have hardened their hearts and do not seek me. It is as it is written.

Many will be amazed at the beauty of my City I have prepared for my bride.

The mansions are of nothing human eyes have seen or can comprehend. Each person will find their hearts desire. Right now, many have no homes and have no crowns.

Shalom.

This is both sad and bittersweet. Many will be rejoicing in Heaven and millions; perhaps billions of people will be suffering in Hell for all their eternity. GOD made the provision to save everyone from the Lake of Fire, but it is by choice whether we accept Jesus into our heart, or if we deny Him. One will be weeping forever, one will be shouting Hallelujah!

> 1 "After this I heard what sounded like the roar of a great multitude in heaven shouting: Hallelujah! Salvation and glory and power belong to our GOD,
> 2 for true and just are His judgments. He has condemned the great prostitute who corrupted the earth by her adulteries. He has avenged on her the blood of His servants."
> 3 And again they shouted: "Hallelujah! The smoke from her goes up for ever and ever."
> 4 The twenty-four elders and the four living creatures fell down and worshiped GOD, who was seated on the throne. And they cried: "Amen, Hallelujah!"
> 5 Then a voice came from the throne, saying: "Praise our GOD, all you His servants, you who fear Him, both small and great!"
> 6 Then I heard what sounded like a great multitude, like the roar of rushing waters and like loud peals of thunder, shouting: "Hallelujah! For our Lord GOD Almighty reigns."
> 7 "Let us rejoice and be glad and give Him glory! For the wedding of the Lamb has come, and His bride has made herself ready.
> 8 Fine linen, bright and clean, was given her to wear." (Fine linen stands for the righteous acts of the Saints.)
> 9 Then the Angel said to me, "Write: 'Blessed are those who are invited to the wedding supper of the Lamb!'" And He added,

"These are the true words of GOD."

¹⁰ At this I fell at His feet to worship Him. But He said to me, "Do not do it! I am a fellow servant with you and with your brothers who hold to the testimony of Jesus. Worship GOD! For the testimony of Jesus is the spirit of prophecy."

The Rider on the White Horse.

¹¹ I saw heaven standing open and there before me was a white horse, whose rider is called Faithful and True. With justice He judges and makes war.

¹² His eyes are like blazing fire, and on His head are many crowns. He has a name written on Him that no one knows but He himself.

¹³ He is dressed in a robe dipped in blood, and His name is the Word of GOD.

¹⁴ The armies of heaven were following Him, riding on white horses and dressed in fine linen, white and clean.

¹⁵ Out of His mouth comes a sharp sword with which to strike down the nations. "He will rule them with an iron scepter." He treads the winepress of the fury of the wrath of GOD Almighty.

¹⁶ On His robe and on His thigh He has this name written: KING OF KINGS AND LORD OF LORDS.

¹⁷ And I saw an Angel standing in the sun, who cried in a loud voice to all the birds flying in midair, "Come, gather together for the great supper of GOD,

¹⁸ so that you may eat the flesh of kings, generals, and mighty men, of horses and their riders, and the flesh of all people, free and slave, small and great."

¹⁹ Then I saw the beast and the kings of the earth and their armies gathered together to make war against the rider on the horse and His army.

²⁰ But the beast was captured, and with him the false prophet who had performed the miraculous signs on his behalf. With these signs he had deluded those who had received the mark

of the beast and worshiped his image. The two of them were thrown alive into the fiery lake of burning sulfur.

²¹ The rest of them were killed with the sword that came out of the mouth of the rider on the horse, and all the birds gorged themselves on their flesh.

Revelation 19 NIV

There will be a final battle and we should observe our lives carefully, so we do not fall and have our flesh gorged by the birds of the air.

As for me and my family, my desire is to be a rider on the white horse in the Army of the Lord and not someone that is slain and forever thrown into the fiery lake of burning sulfur.

I understand by studying Revelation that after the previous Chapter, those who have been beheaded because of their testimony for Jesus, and because they had not worshiped the beast or his image, nor had they received the mark of the beast on their forehead or right hand, these are the ones that will come to life and reign with Christ a thousand years.

After this thousand year period, the rest of the dead will rise for the final White Throne Judgment. Those who are saved by believing on Jesus Christ will then be dwelling in the Heavenly City for all eternity.

Please know that we will all stand before the Judgment Seat of Christ, where our eternal destination is pronounced, just as in a modern day court of law.

The difference however is monumental; there are no appeals! Once judgment is made, there are no more chances to change your eternal destination.

The Thousand Years.

¹ And I saw an Angel coming down out of heaven, having the key to the Abyss and holding in his hand a great chain.

² He seized the dragon, that ancient serpent, who is the devil, or Satan, and bound him for a thousand years.

³ He threw him into the Abyss, and locked and sealed it over him, to keep him from deceiving the nations anymore until the thousand years were ended. After that, he must be set free for a short time.

⁴ I saw thrones on which were seated those who had been given authority to judge. And I saw the souls of those who had been beheaded because of their testimony for Jesus and because of the word of GOD. They had not worshiped the beast or his image and had not received his mark on their foreheads or their hands. They came to life and reigned with Christ a thousand years.

⁵ (The rest of the dead did not come to life until the thousand years were ended.) This is the first resurrection.

⁶ Blessed and holy are those who have part in the first resurrection. The second death has no power over them, but they will be priests of GOD and of Christ and will reign with Him for a thousand years.

⁷ When the thousand years are over, Satan will be released from his prison,

⁸ and will go out to deceive the nations in the four corners of the earth, Gog and Magog, to gather them for battle. In number they are like the sand on the seashore.

⁹ They marched across the breadth of the earth and surrounded the camp of GOD's people, the city He loves. But fire came down from heaven and devoured them.

¹⁰ And the devil, who deceived them, was thrown into the lake of burning sulfur, where the beast and the false prophet had been thrown. They will be tormented day and night for ever and ever.

¹¹ Then I saw a great white throne and Him who was seated on it. Earth and sky fled from His presence, and there was no place for them.

¹² And I saw the dead, great and small, standing before the throne, and books were opened. Another book was opened, which is the Book of Life. The dead were judged according to what they had done as recorded in the books.

¹³ The sea gave up the dead that were in it, and death and Hades gave up the dead that were in them, and each person was judged according to what he had done.

¹⁴ Then death and Hades were thrown into the Lake of Fire. The Lake of Fire is the second death.

¹⁵ If anyone's name was not found written in the Book of Life, he was thrown into the Lake of Fire.

Revelation 20 NIV

As we have read above, the Holy and Righteous will dwell with Jesus for all eternity. Sadly, the evil and unrighteous will suffer tremendously for all eternity.

Heaven will be filled with peace and united will be everyone who takes part in the marriage supper of the Lamb.

We will be as one, married to Jesus Christ Himself and we will never be sad, lonely or forgotten, ever again. We will continuously sing praises to His name forever and forevermore.

The purest of love we have never known will be in Heaven.

My grandfather, Buddy Elmer Null experienced death, but returned to life. His heart stopped for over ten minutes, while he was suffering a heart attack in the hospital. He saw the doctors and nurses working on his body, he watched as they ran around trying to restart his heartbeat. During that time, my grandfather experienced what many others who have been in this same situation experience.

As he was recounting his experience with me, he didn't even realize that others had experienced similar experiences, and he was so enthusiastic in telling me of this event, in vivid detail.

I was only a teenager, but it seems like it was just yesterday when he told me, "Windy, don't ever be afraid to die."

My grandfather felt a pull on his spirit as he went floating out of his body and into this very, very bright light. He had never seen anything so brilliant in his life.

He said he felt the most incredible love, like he had never experienced before!

Then he saw something familiar, his mother coming out to him and he saw the gate of Heaven. He said it was magnificent! He was overwhelmed with joy and then it was gone. He wanted to reach for his mother so badly, but the next thing he knew, his eyes were opening back up in the hospital room, in that decaying body of his that was suffering with Parkinson's disease.

He was angry and upset to be back in his body. He wanted to go home to Jesus.

Several years later my grandfather did pass away. I was by his side and holding his hand, along with my precious mother. He hated leaving us behind, but I told him to "go home" and be free from the pain he dealt with in his body every day.

I know he is in heaven and I know he had given his life to Jesus Christ when he was a young boy.

He was a quiet man, who never attended Church much, but he loved the Lord. He was a quiet servant and his love for his family was pure. I know that GOD gave me my grandfather to show me how much He loves me. His life was a testimony of simple living and he walked what he talked. He was a simple man, who loved to widdel on branches off of trees and spit chewing tobacco and brag about his "blondie," who is my mom and his only child.

I know that my grandfather is with Jesus and that assurance has carried me through the grief. For me, knowing your loved ones are with Jesus Christ is the most calming and amazing reassurance you can carry inside when the grief of loss wants to take over your emotions.

That is why, no matter the difficulty, we should all strive to tell our unsaved friends, neighbors, co-workers and families about the sacrifice of Jesus and how much HE loves them! Jesus loves you and me so much and experiencing the grief of loss can be overwhelming.

Don't put off another day to tell someone you love about Jesus. If they reject Him, rest assured that your work was not in vain. Their blood will not be on your hands on Judgment Day and you can mourn them knowing you did tell them about Jesus.

[1] Jude, a servant of Jesus Christ and a brother of James; to those who have been called, who are loved by GOD the Father and kept by Jesus Christ:
[2] Mercy, peace and love be yours in abundance.

The sin and doom of Godless men.

³ Dear friends, although I was very eager to write to you about the salvation we share, I felt I had to write and urge you to contend for the faith that was once for all entrusted to the Saints.

⁴ For certain men whose condemnation was written about long ago have secretly slipped in among you. They are godless men, who change the grace of our GOD into a license for immorality and deny Jesus Christ our only Sovereign and Lord.

⁵ Though you already know all this, I want to remind you that the Lord delivered His people out of Egypt, but later destroyed those who did not believe.

⁶ And the Angels who did not keep their positions of authority, but abandoned their own home, these He has kept in darkness, bound with everlasting chains for judgment on the great Day.

⁷ In a similar way, Sodom and Gomorrah and the surrounding towns gave themselves up to sexual immorality and perversion. They serve as an example of those who suffer the punishment of eternal fire.

⁸ In the very same way, these dreamers pollute their own bodies, reject authority and slander celestial beings.

⁹ But even the Archangel Michael, when he was disputing with the devil about the body of Moses, did not dare to bring a slanderous accusation against him, but said, "The Lord rebuke you!"

¹⁰ Yet these men speak abusively against whatever they do not understand; and what things they do understand by instinct, like unreasoning animals these are the very things that destroy them.

¹¹ Woe to them! They have taken the way of Cain; they have rushed for profit into Balaam's error; they have been destroyed in Korah's rebellion.

¹² These men are blemishes at your love feasts, eating with you without the slightest qualm, shepherds who feed only themselves. They are clouds without rain, blown along by the wind; autumn trees, without fruit and uprooted, twice dead.

¹³ They are wild waves of the sea, foaming up their shame; wandering stars, for whom blackest darkness has been reserved forever.

¹⁴ Enoch, the seventh from Adam, prophesied about these men: "See, the Lord is coming with thousands upon thousands of His holy ones,

¹⁵ to judge everyone, and to convict all the ungodly of all the ungodly acts they have done in the ungodly way, and of all the harsh words ungodly sinners have spoken against him."

¹⁶ These men are grumblers and faultfinders; they follow their own evil desires; they boast about themselves and flatter others for their own advantage.

A call to Persevere.

¹⁷ But, dear friends, remember what the apostles of our Lord Jesus Christ foretold.

¹⁸ They said to you, "In the last times there will be scoffers who will follow their own ungodly desires."

¹⁹ These are the men who divide you, who follow mere natural instincts and do not have the Spirit.

²⁰ But you, dear friends, build yourselves up in your most holy faith and pray in the Holy Spirit.

²¹ Keep yourselves in GOD's love as you wait for the mercy of our Lord Jesus Christ to bring you to eternal life.

²² Be merciful to those who doubt;

²³ snatch others from the fire and save them; to others show mercy, mixed with fear, hating even the clothing stained by corrupted flesh.

Doxology.

²⁴ To Him, who is able to keep you from falling and to present you before His glorious presence without fault and with great joy,

²⁵ to the only GOD our Savior be glory, majesty, power and authority, through Jesus Christ our Lord, before all ages, now and forevermore! Amen.

Jude 1 NIV

Dwelling in His presence is fullness of joy beyond measure and the atmosphere will be filled with the singing and praising of our King of Kings and Lord of Lords, Jesus Christ, the Father GOD and the spirits of GOD, all dwelling in unity for an eternity.

I can dream of the beauty that will be found behind those pearly gates.

The Heavenly City will be surrounded by twelve gates, each formed out of one pearl. Can you imagine how magnificent the pearls will be to adorn an entire gate?

Behind these city gates we will be filled with wonder at the beautiful and magnificent structures, shimmering in much color, akin to a transparency type illusion of color. Every color in the rainbow will be represented and in all things.

Buildings will be multi-faceted, just as GOD is. The streets are poured before your feet, glimmering as pure gold.

The New Jerusalem.

> ¹ Then I saw a new heaven and a new earth, for the first heaven and the first earth had passed away, and there was no longer any sea.
> ² I saw the Holy City, the New Jerusalem, coming down out of heaven from GOD, prepared as a bride beautifully dressed for her husband.
> ³ And I heard a loud voice from the throne saying, "Now the dwelling of GOD is with men, and He will live with them. They will be His people, and GOD Himself will be with them and be their GOD.
> ⁴ He will wipe every tear from their eyes. There will be no more death or mourning or crying or pain, for the old order of things has passed away."

⁵ He who was seated on the throne said, "I am making everything new!" Then He said, "Write this down, for these words are trustworthy and true."

⁶ He said to me: "It is done. I am the Alpha and the Omega, the Beginning and the End. To him who is thirsty I will give to drink without cost from the spring of the water of life.

⁷ He who overcomes will inherit all this, and I will be his GOD and he will be my Son.

⁸ But the cowardly, the unbelieving, the vile, the murderers, the sexually immoral, those who practice magic arts, the idolaters and all liars, their place will be in the fiery lake of burning sulfur. This is the second death."

⁹ One of the seven Angels who had the seven bowls full of the seven last plagues came and said to me, "Come, I will show you the bride, the wife of the Lamb."

¹⁰ And He carried me away in the Spirit to a mountain great and high, and showed me the Holy City, Jerusalem, coming down out of heaven from GOD.

¹¹ It shone with the glory of GOD, and its brilliance was like that of a very precious jewel, like a jasper, clear as crystal.

¹² It had a great, high wall with twelve gates and with twelve Angels at the gates. On the gates were written the names of the twelve tribes of Israel.

¹³ There were three gates on the east, three on the north, three on the south and three on the west.

¹⁴ The wall of the city had twelve foundations, and on them were the names of the twelve apostles of the Lamb.

¹⁵ The Angel who talked with me had a measuring rod of gold to measure the city, its gates and its walls.

¹⁶ The city was laid out like a square, as long as it was wide. He measured the City with the rod and found it to be 12,000 stadia in length, and as wide and high as it is long.

¹⁷ He measured its wall and it was 144 cubits thick, by man's measurement, which the Angel was using.

¹⁸ The wall was made of jasper, and the City of pure gold, as pure as glass.

¹⁹ The foundations of the City walls were decorated with every kind of precious stone. The first foundation was jasper, the second sapphire, the third chalcedony, the fourth emerald,
²⁰ the fifth sardonyx, the sixth carnelian, the seventh chrysolite, the eighth beryl, the ninth topaz, the tenth chrysoprase, the eleventh jacinth, and the twelfth amethyst.
²¹ The twelve gates were twelve pearls, each gate made of a single pearl. The great street of the City was of pure gold, like transparent glass.
²² I did not see a temple in the City, because the Lord GOD Almighty and the Lamb are its temple.
²³ The city does not need the sun or the moon to shine on it, for the glory of GOD gives it light, and the Lamb is its lamp.
²⁴ The nations will walk by its light, and the kings of the earth will bring their splendor into it.
²⁵ On no day will its gates ever be shut, for there will be no night there.
²⁶ The glory and honor of the nations will be brought into it.
²⁷ Nothing impure will ever enter it, nor will anyone who does what is shameful or deceitful, but only those whose names are written in the Lamb's Book of Life.

Revelation 21 NIV

The River of Life.

¹ Then the Angel showed me the river of the water of life, as clear as crystal, flowing from the throne of GOD and of the Lamb,
² down the middle of the great street of the City. On each side of the river stood the tree of life, bearing twelve crops of fruit, yielding its fruit every month. And the leaves of the tree are for the healing of the nations.
³ No longer will there be any curse. The throne of GOD and of the Lamb will be in the City, and His servants will serve Him.
⁴ They will see His face, and His name will be on their foreheads.
⁵ There will be no more night. They will not need the light of a lamp or the light of the sun, for the Lord GOD will give them light. And they will reign for ever and ever.

⁶The Angel said to me, "These words are trustworthy and true. The Lord, the GOD of the spirits of the prophets, sent His Angel to show His servants the things that must soon take place."

Jesus Is Coming.

⁷"Behold, I am coming soon! Blessed is he who keeps the words of the prophecy in this book."

⁸I, John, am the one who heard and saw these things. And when I had heard and seen them, I fell down to worship at the feet of the Angel who had been showing them to me.

⁹But he said to me, "Do not do it! I am a fellow servant with you and with your brothers the prophets and of all who keep the words of this book. Worship GOD!"

¹⁰Then he told me, "Do not seal up the words of the prophecy of this book, because the time is near.

¹¹Let him who does wrong continue to do wrong; let him who is vile continue to be vile; let him who does right continue to do right; and let him who is holy continue to be holy."

¹²"Behold, I am coming soon! My reward is with me, and I will give to everyone according to what he has done.

¹³I am the Alpha and the Omega, the First and the Last, the Beginning and the End."

¹⁴"Blessed are those who wash their robes, that they may have the right to the tree of life and may go through the gates into the City.

¹⁵Outside are the dogs, those who practice magic arts, the sexually immoral, the murderers, the idolaters and everyone who loves and practices falsehood."

¹⁶"I, Jesus, have sent my Angel to give you this testimony for the Churches. I am the Root and the Offspring of David, and the bright Morning Star."

¹⁷The Spirit and the bride say, "Come!" And let him who hears say, "Come!" Whoever is thirsty, let him come; and whoever wishes, let him take the free gift of the water of life.

[18] I warn everyone who hears the words of the prophecy of this book: If anyone adds anything to them, GOD will add to him the plagues described in this book.
[19] And if anyone takes words away from this book of prophecy, GOD will take away from him his share in the tree of life and in the holy city, which are described in this book.
[20] He who testifies to these things says, "Yes, I am coming soon." Amen. Come, Lord Jesus.
[21] The grace of the Lord Jesus be with GOD's people. Amen.

Revelation 22 NIV

What magnificent light there will be and the Son of GOD will be the source of light for all eternity. I am patiently waiting for the day when I will be with the Lord forevermore.

Are you looking forward to dwelling with GOD in the Heavenly City, the New Jerusalem?

Epilogue

The Bible states in John, Chapter 10:27 (KJV) that "my sheep hear my voice" and today He is still speaking to us!

Jesus Christ is the same yesterday, today and forever. He does not change like the shifting shadows and He will meet our every need, but we must come to Him with a repentant heart and lay down our lives so He can truly give us life abundantly.

> 22 Then came the Feast of Dedication at Jerusalem. It was winter,
> 23 and Jesus was in the temple area walking in Solomon's Colonnade.
> 24 The Jews gathered around Him, saying, "How long will you keep us in suspense? If you are the Christ, tell us plainly."
> 25 Jesus answered, "I did tell you, but you do not believe. The miracles I do in my Father's name speak for me,
> 26 but you do not believe because you are not my sheep.
> 27 My sheep listen to my voice; I know them, and they follow me.
> 28 I give them eternal life, and they shall never perish; no one can snatch them out of my hand.
> 29 My Father, who has given them to me, is greater than all; no one can snatch them out of my Father's hand.
> 30 I and the Father are one."
>
> John 10:22-29 NIV

Would you like to be one with the Father and Jesus Christ? Have you suffered in your life long enough without Jesus Christ?

Christ suffered to bring us eternal life and in His suffering, He condemned the world and the sin that hinders our daily walk. We can live victoriously and we can have a future of hope. We can make a difference in our world, each and every day!

Would you like to ask Jesus Christ into your heart and live with You?

Repeat this simple prayer and I assure you that Jesus will come into your heart and forgive you of all your sins, if you truly mean it.

"Lord Jesus, I know that I am a Sinner and that I need you in my life. Jesus, come into my heart and forgive me of all my sins. Help me to live for you. I acknowledge that you are truly the Son of GOD and the only way through which I can be saved. Lord, I believe, save me Lord Jesus. Amen."

If you have given your heart to Jesus Christ please tell others so they can rejoice with you! Please send me a note; I would love to hear from you!

My website address is: www.artcetra.net.

One by one, with each person living a life surrendered to Jesus Christ, we will become a person whose desire is not to harm each other, but to live in unity for a better tomorrow. One heart pure and full of love, which is my hope and my dream for the world we live in!

Each of us can make a difference in our world. Won't you?

The Workers Are Few.

> [35] Jesus went through all the towns and villages, teaching in their synagogues, preaching the good news of the kingdom and healing every disease and sickness.
> [36] When He saw the crowds, He had compassion on them, because they were harassed and helpless, like sheep without a shepherd.
> [37] Then He said to His disciples, "The harvest is plentiful but the workers are few.

^{38} Ask the Lord of the harvest, therefore, to send out workers into His harvest field."

Matthew 9:35-38 NIV

I am only one person, doing what GOD has called me to do, but hopefully in my humble attempts to fulfill the calling on my life, someone will give their life to Jesus Christ and will make a difference in their world for others.

I encourage everyone reading this book, to listen for the voice of GOD and know that it is possible to hear Him, if we will open our hearts and minds to Him.

If you didn't pray to receive Jesus Christ as your Savior, it will be most difficult, if not impossible, to hear the voice of GOD.

Please put your trust in Jesus, He doesn't need you to be perfect, you are worthy of His love just as you are!

Sadly, we can be saved in our heads and not in our hearts. Therefore, we will miss Heaven by about 15 inches and what a tragedy that will be!

I don't want anyone missing Heaven and I cannot imagine my life without Jesus Christ, who speaks to me.

GOD does not want YOU to end up in Hell and this is the sole reason for all these messages He keeps equipping me with, just as in the one below.

May 14, 2005
3:00 a.m.

My beloved,

There are many things I want to share with you, yet everything must come in my timing, which is my perfect will for you.

Many upon the earth have a false sense of who I am. Many will unknowingly perish in the Lake of Fire, even though they have works of serving me. Their deeds were all in vain. Many are blinded by the truth and you live in a selfish and uncaring world full of greed and hatred, the love of most has waxed cold.

That is why you were sent at such a time as this. To snatch many from the fiery pit of hell, and to set their feet on the right path. So many misunderstand me. I do not desire for any to perish, but their own hardened hearts make it impossible for me to save them. I am not a man that I should lie, yet it breaks my heart that so many do not understand.

My ways are higher than their ways and I dwell in everlasting light, there is not darkness, so all is revealed in my presence. Those who bask in my presence have the fullness of joy and receive power and revelation and a sound mind.

My anointing is upon your life and those who are in your presence will feel my presence. Keep showing my love to the world, prove me in this, I will give you the desires of your heart, for you are my beloved Carla, and I love you with an everlasting love.

Shalom.

Please, give your heart to Jesus Christ and then go find your secret place to sit in silence, where you will learn the deeper things of life from Him, our maker and creator and you will hear the voice of GOD.

A Song of Praise

> [1] In that day this song will be sung in the land of Judah: We have a strong city; GOD makes salvation its walls and ramparts.
> [2] Open the gates that the righteous nation may enter, the nation that keeps faith.
> [3] You will keep in perfect peace him whose mind is steadfast, because he trusts in you.
> [4] Trust in the LORD forever, for the LORD, the LORD, is the Rock eternal.
> [5] He humbles those who dwell on high; He lays the lofty city low; He levels it to the ground and casts it down to the dust.
> [6] Feet trample it down, the feet of the oppressed, the footsteps of the poor.

⁷ The path of the righteous is level; O upright One, you make the way of the righteous smooth.
⁸ Yes, LORD, walking in the way of your laws; we wait for you; your name and renown are the desire of our hearts.
⁹ My soul yearns for you in the night; in the morning my spirit longs for you. When your judgments come upon the earth, the people of the world learn righteousness.
¹⁰ Though grace is shown to the wicked, they do not learn righteousness; even in a land of uprightness they go on doing evil and regard not the majesty of the LORD.
¹¹ O LORD, your hand is lifted high, but they do not see it. Let them see your zeal for your people and be put to shame; let the fire reserved for your enemies consume them.
¹² LORD, you establish peace for us; all that we have accomplished you have done for us.
¹³ O LORD, our GOD, other lords besides you have ruled over us, but your name alone do we honor.
¹⁴ They are now dead, they live no more; those departed spirits do not rise. You punished them and brought them to ruin; you wiped out all memory of them.
¹⁵ You have enlarged the nation, O LORD; you have enlarged the nation. You have gained glory for yourself; you have extended all the borders of the land.
¹⁶ LORD, they came to you in their distress; when you disciplined them, they could barely whisper a prayer.
¹⁷ As a woman with child and about to give birth writhes and cries out in her pain, so were we in your presence, O LORD.
¹⁸ We were with child, we writhed in pain, but we gave birth to wind. We have not brought salvation to the earth; we have not given birth to people of the world.
¹⁹ But your dead will live; their bodies will rise. You, who dwell in the dust, wake up and shout for joy. Your dew is like the dew of the morning; the earth will give birth to her dead.
²⁰ Go, my people, enter your rooms and shut the doors behind you; hide yourselves for a little while until His wrath has passed by.

[21] See the LORD is coming out of His dwelling to punish the people of the earth for their sins. The earth will disclose the blood shed upon her; she will conceal her slain no longer.

Isaiah 26 NIV

Take heed to these words and give your life to Jesus Christ!

He is the Prince of Peace and He will walk with you through your shadows of death and no lasting harm will come to you. Trust Jesus Christ as your Savior and walk with Him today!

Remember, it is your choice to believe and to receive, healing, wholeness and salvation from Jesus Christ, who never changes and HE is no respecter of persons!

There are countless people who have been healed, delivered and set free from the bondages of life and since He has set them free, He can and will set you free!

I know, I was once a very lost Sinner, who was destructive and hurting. I was demon-possessed and walked for 43 years being oppressed, sick and suicidal, and then Jesus set me free!

He set me free and He wants to do the same for your life!

Please don't close this book and lay it on a shelf, without letting HIS love find your heart and open it. You are worthy of HIS salvation and it is yours for the taking!

GOD BLESSES YOU, accept HIS BLESSINGS!

Shalom and peace be with you always!

Carla J. Akin
www.artcetra.net

Final Words for Thought

February 19, 2005
3:30 a.m.

Show them my love for them! They are my children and my heart's cry is that none should perish. Oh how lost are the multitudes, they don't listen for my voice, my Holy Spirit cannot contend with them. So few seek me!

My wrath is coming, I will not delay. Warn the people!

I have chosen you from the foundation of the earth and I love you. You are mine; I am a jealous GOD, a consuming fire! You cannot quench me; I am alive and ever living.

Depart from all evil, have nothing to do with the doctrines of the devil; don't be enticed by the enemy. You are in a battle, seek me and stay and abide in me. Do not look to the left or the right. My mercy endureth forever.

I will direct your path, do not question, but obey and follow me.

Shalom.

Other books by the Author:

Competing With the Shadow

Printed in the United States
46896LVS00008B/184-225